Managing Digital
Audiovisual Resources

PRACTICAL GUIDES FOR LIBRARIANS

About the Series

This innovative series written and edited for librarians by librarians provides authoritative, practical information and guidance on a wide spectrum of library processes and operations.

Books in the series are focused, describing practical and innovative solutions to a problem facing today's librarian and delivering step-by-step guidance for planning, creating, implementing, managing, and evaluating a wide range of services and programs.

The books are aimed at beginning and intermediate librarians needing basic instruction/guidance in a specific subject and at experienced librarians who need to gain knowledge in a new area or guidance in implementing a new program/service.

About the Series Editor

The **Practical Guides for Librarians** series was conceived by and is edited by M. Sandra Wood, MLS, MBA, AHIP, FMLA, Librarian Emerita, Penn State University Libraries.

M. Sandra Wood was a librarian at the George T. Harrell Library, The Milton S. Hershey Medical Center, College of Medicine, Pennsylvania State University, Hershey, PA, for over 35 years, specializing in reference, educational, and database services. Ms. Wood worked for several years as a Development Editor for Neal-Schuman Publishers.

Ms. Wood received a MLS from Indiana University and a MBA from the University of Maryland. She is a Fellow of the Medical Library Association and served as a member of MLA's Board of Directors from 1991 to 1995. Ms. Wood is founding and current editor of *Medical Reference Services Quarterly*, now in its 35th volume. She also was founding editor of the *Journal of Consumer Health on the Internet* and the *Journal of Electronic Resources in Medical Libraries* and served as editor/co-editor of both journals through 2011.

Titles in the Series

1. *How to Teach: A Practical Guide for Librarians* by Beverley E. Crane.

2. *Implementing an Inclusive Staffing Model for Today's Reference Services* by Julia K. Nims, Paula Storm, and Robert Stevens.

3. *Managing Digital Audiovisual Resources: A Practical Guide for Librarians* by Matthew C. Mariner.

Managing Digital Audiovisual Resources

A Practical Guide for Librarians

Matthew C. Mariner

PRACTICAL GUIDES FOR LIBRARIANS, NO. 3

ROWMAN & LITTLEFIELD
Lanham • Boulder • New York • Toronto • Plymouth, UK

Published by Rowman & Littlefield
4501 Forbes Boulevard, Suite 200, Lanham, Maryland 20706
www.rowman.com

10 Thornbury Road, Plymouth PL6 7PP, United Kingdom

British Library Cataloguing in Publication Information Available

Library of Congress Cataloging-in-Publication Data

Mariner, Matthew C., 1984–
    Managing digital audiovisual resources : a practical guide for librarians / Matthew C. Mariner.
        pages cm. — (Practical guides for librarians ; no. 3)
    Includes bibliographical references and index.
    ISBN 978-0-8108-9103-6 (pbk. : alk. paper) — ISBN 978-0-8108-9104-3 (ebook)
    1. Libraries—Special collections—Audio-visual materials. 2. Audio-visual materials—
Digitization. I. Title.
    Z692.A93M37 2014
    025.17'7—dc23   2013040159

This book is dedicated to several persons and creatures.
First to my awesomely supportive and patient wife, Dina,
who reminds me constantly that I'm no dummy.
Second to my parents, John and Jude,
who knew without doubt I'd eventually write something worthwhile.
Third to my two hilarious cats, Ivan and Betts,
who snuggled me while I wrote this book.
And finally I dedicate this book to my brother, Zach,
who won't get to read it but who would have been the first to finish.

Contents

List of Illustrations

⊚ Figures

⦿ Tables

List of Textboxes

Preface

While working as a digital library technologist at the University of Florida, I was often faced with challenges in digitizing odd physical formats. Antique maps, miniature books, and three-dimensional objects all posed unique challenges. Typically, I was prepared to make informed judgments and had at my disposal most of the tools necessary to digitize such oddities. As my department began to field more and more requests for audiovisual digitization, it became clear that not all the tools and expertise that I had in imaging were applicable. I tasked myself with assembling new arrays of equipment and creating unique workflows and processes from scratch. Without the support of my colleagues and a smattering of Internet resources, I would not have been able to succeed in this new venture. What was missing from my toolkit, though, was a single guidebook relevant to digitizing and managing audiovisual resources specific to persons in the library world. Such a guide would have helped to stabilize those first shaky steps and elucidate the then-mysterious trials of audiovisual digitization.

Managing Digital Audiovisual Resources: A Practical Guide for Librarians takes a practical approach to informing librarians, or allied professionals in various library sectors, on how to take a measured, efficient, and informed approach to audiovisual digitization projects and programs. As is the case with most literature on the subject of audiovisual engineering and digitization, this book does not cover every facet of the field—and there are many—but it does lay a solid foundation for building a much larger silo of information. This guide can be used to direct the planning, implementation, and continued support of an audiovisual digitization project, but it does not assume deep foreknowledge of the subject, nor does it demand total absorption from one concept to the next.

Digitization projects require skills and input from all kinds of information professionals, not just librarians. With this in mind, it would be wise to share the contents of this book with all persons involved in a project regardless of their professions. *Managing Digital Audiovisual Resources* takes readers from collections assessment before digitization all the way to figuring out what to do once material has been converted. Processes, workflows, tables, and technology capsules are located throughout, offering readers digestible snippets of information easily decontextualized and applicable in a variety of scenarios. By the end of the book, readers should be familiar with the following:

- The makeup of the audiovisual collection, physically and content-wise
- The differences between analog and digital formats

- Crafting a collection development policy
- Determining an audience for digital projects
- Planning and copyright
- Working with digitization vendors
- Starting in-house digitization from scratch
- Selecting presentation and repository technologies

Managing Digital Audiovisual Resources is composed of eight chapters that lead readers from the most basic concepts in audiovisual digitization to higher-level discussions of purpose and intent. Chapter 1, "The Basics of Managing Digital Audiovisual Resources," introduces the basic concepts that a person must grasp to begin a digitization project of any size. These concepts include understanding collections, users, and products, which will inform most other decisions later in a project. Chapter 2, "What Do You Have? Evaluating Collections," instructs readers on how to determine what makes their collections special. File formats, material content, and other aspects of collection description are addressed in detail.

Collection assessment and evaluation are approached from a different perspective in chapter 3. "Evaluating Collections: Picking a Direction and Developing Collections" discusses the necessity for librarians to determine the size, scope, and focus of current resources, as well as a viable path for future development. This is important in the longevity and sustainable relevance of a collection. As a basis of understanding collections is established, readers enter chapter 4, "Planning for Digitization." This chapter asks readers to consider their current capabilities for digitizing materials and making them available to users in a meaningful way. "Planning for Digitization" also explores ways in which librarians can increase the value of a project through collaboration.

Process, workflows, and equipment considerations are addressed in detail in chapter 5, "Digitization: Managing Digitization, Selecting Equipment, and Applying Standards." Readers are advised on how to logically approach digitization and whether to pursue an in-house program or the services of vendors. Chapter 6, "Presentation and Access," provides an overview of the tools that a librarian can wield to provide access for digitized resources. After materials are digitized, they must be presented to an audience, often in perpetuity, and this chapter guides readers through the process of determining the most appropriate presentation and access technologies.

In chapter 7, "Enhancement and Promotion," suggestions are made for ways to improve the usability and appeal of published digital projects. Focusing some amount of effort on the appearance and usability of a digital project will go a long way in ensuring its longevity and continued relevance. Finally, chapter 8, "Essential Takeaways," concludes the book with a review of major points and directs readers to other valuable resources in the field of audiovisual digitization and management.

These subjects and much more are covered from a top-down perspective, beginning at ideal starting points but still considering real-life roadblocks. It should not be assumed that the answers to all issues that might arise during a project are in this book, but if answers are not found here, this book points out other resources that likely will have answers. The most important thing to remember about audiovisual digitization is that many other librarians, archivists, and allied professionals have experienced the very same issues and even more have applicable solutions. This book should be used as a jumping-off point for further explorations in the world of audiovisual conversion and, certainly, as just one of many tools available to the keen researcher. With this book in hand, a little confidence, and the willingness to try, any librarian can embark upon a successful digitization project.

Acknowledgments

There are several individuals and entities that I would like to thank for assisting me, even indirectly, in the composition of this book. First I would like to thank the directors of Auraria Library, who have made it a point to vehemently support the research activities of faculty. Without their support and encouragement, I would never have found the time to write a book. I would also like to thank my colleagues at Auraria Library for being supportive and interested. Among them are Jeffrey Beall, Rosemary Evetts, Meg Brown-Sica, Denise Pan, Liz Cooper, Leslie Williams, and Dr. Mary Somerville.

I would like to thank the digital library community at large, which excels and innovates in an industry with no goal other than the free and unhindered dissemination of knowledge. It is because of digital librarians, archivists, and support staff that our accumulated cultures, histories, and intellectual outputs will be around for centuries. Specifically, I would like to thank the Internet Archive, an organization self-charged with the preservation of all manner of human creation and one that asks for little in return other than curiosity.

Most important, I would like to acknowledge the staff and faculty of the University of Florida Digital Library Center. It was in the center that I first cut my teeth on audiovisual digitization. The seven years that I spent at the University of Florida was an invaluable experience, without which I would not have had the experience to write an entire book about practical audiovisual digitization. Specifically, I would like to thank Dr. Laurie Taylor, Randall Renner, Will Canova, Mark Sullivan, Traveler Wendell, Lourdes Santamaria-Wheeler, Jane "Jen" Pen, Tabatha Sullivan, Dina Mariner, James Barnett, Joe Kaleita, Gus Clifton, Stephanie Haas, and Erich Kesse.

Finally, I would like to thank my editor, M. Sandra Wood. Her expert patience in dealing with a first-time author was appreciated. Without her direction, I would not have felt as though I had completed something valuable to my profession.

CHAPTER 1

The Basics of Managing Digital Audiovisual Resources

IN THIS CHAPTER

▷ Understanding collections

▷ Understanding users

▷ Understanding products

THERE ARE HUNDREDS OF COMPONENTS to any successful digitization program or project, often more than what many persons expect. This is true of any intrinsically complex effort, but in audiovisual digitization, it is compounded by the mysteries of legacy playback equipment, such as U-Matic videocassette players; the mystery of getting content trapped on obsolete media to something modern and widely usable; and the mystery of how exactly to manage it all. It is difficult to translate to videos and audios the skills that a person might have in photographing or digitizing print materials such as rare books or manuscripts, especially since such objects are still readable and usable by most users in their current form. Audiovisual materials such as Betamax cassettes and reel-to-reel tape contain "readable" information but cannot be used without an intermediary. We read books with our eyes but must rely on second-party devices to interpret the information on videocassettes and other multimedia objects. This is the complicating condition in managing audiovisual resources and can be the most intimidating.

There is no reason for complicating factors to deter librarians, archivists, and other information professionals from confidently pursuing audiovisual digitization projects. The information stored—trapped in some cases—on functionally obsolete media could be just as important to researchers as any obviously valuable object, such as an antique map or rare book. The biggest hurdle to overcome is not any of the aforementioned mysteries but a shroud of misunderstanding covering the essentially familiar concepts in converting analog media to digital. Librarians do not need to be audiovisual engineers to execute and manage these concepts; they simply need to connect with informational resources and other librarians and professionals with experience in digitizing audiovisual materials.

Basic Concepts

There are far too many concepts inherent in any digitization project system to iterate in a single volume, but most can be congealed into a simplified trio. If remembered, these three major concepts can be picked apart, trifurcated, and reapplied with any other convenient metric or intention:

- Understanding collections
- Understanding users
- Understanding products

These concepts can be addressed in any order. A firm grip on the foundation of audiovisual digitization can be grasped by understanding collections, users, and products. In this context, "understanding" should be defined as knowledge of the traits and needs of a given subject.

Understanding Collections

Collections consist of anything from a handful of audiocassette tapes to dozens of boxes of 35-mm motion picture films in canisters. More likely than a range of single-item types, though, will be collections composed of a mix of media: U-Matic videocassettes, reel-to-reel audiotape, 16-mm motion picture film, and, the most common medium, VHS videocassettes. The traits of each audiovisual medium differ and the media themselves almost always require dedicated hardware.

For example, U-Matic videocassettes will not play on VHS videocassette recorders; Betamax tapes will not play in Betacam decks; and one film gauge will not necessarily play in the projector for another. Thus, librarians can look at the understanding of collections as the attainment of familiarity with the traits and needs of different media (e.g., the shape and the device required to accommodate it). From these traits and needs, librarians can determine the type of equipment that they need to capture and digitize content, and they will be able to restrict a program's boundaries appropriately.

Understanding a collection can also mean knowing the kinds of content held in each object. This level of familiarity may be harder than simply figuring out what types of media are owned, as tapes are not always intuitively labeled and, unlike books, such materials cannot simply be "read." To be sure, technological understanding must precede subjectival understanding. Once the objects can be replayed and reviewed, a person can determine the subject matter of the content (e.g., archival films of homecoming day parades). When the content is understood, then a project manager can determine the users who might be interested in such things.

Understanding Users

Users are those individuals or groups of persons that find some value in the materials digitized and presented through a project. Users or audiences can be from an interested segment, such as biology professors or graduate students, or they can simply be the general public. With a wide-enough array of material, any project can be deemed usable by all persons regardless of affiliation, but most digitization projects are started with a certain set or subset of the population in mind. Such tailoring helps limit the overall cost of a project while leaving its expansion up for interpretation.

Understanding users also brings with it insight into how to best promote and expose the final result of a project. One of the biggest problems with library resources is the lackadaisical way in which promotion is approached, if it is approached at all. One way to do this is to digitize a collection of VHS tapes and tell everyone at the host university or institution that Collection X is now digitized and online. This is not very effective or efficient, as it assumes that blanketing a campus with paper- or Internet-based promotional imagery is going to attract more than just the casual observer.

When a librarian knows in detail the kinds of people who will likely be interested in a resource, she or he can more easily seek out such individuals. Such targeting will open up excellent opportunities, for example, the integration of resources into a course. If resources are integrated into a course or made a necessary part of a variety of courses, it establishes the resources as essential and all but ensures their longevity. The only issue at that point is the final product of a project. While several courses may demand yearly use of a set of digitized resources, the usability of a collection of digital videos may not be possible in perpetuity. Demand must be buttressed by functionality and sustainability.

Understanding Products

The products of a digitization project can be the digital files accumulated during conversion or the ways in which those files are presented to users, as in streaming media systems or digital repositories. Both the file formats and the presentation settings must be either sustainable or easy to migrate from one platform to another. The former—perpetual certainty—is highly unlikely. File format standards and preferences change every few years, and no information professional should assume that his or her preferred format would reign supreme. Furthermore, as viewing technologies change and the preferences of users shift, librarians must accommodate not their own desires but those of their constituents, even if those desires run counter to set standards.

The platforms in which resources are stored and presented to constituents (streaming media systems or digital repositories) are just as likely to fall out of favor or technological ingenuity as the formats they store. This constant of change is simply something for which project managers must account when designing a project or program. The most important thing, ultimately, is to take time and put forth effort to monitor changes in preference and technology so that no project ever becomes a static reminder of poor planning. This is easier said than done, though, as even excellent planning can be overmatched by completely divergent shifts in technology and favor.

The notion that technology is now such that formats will be mutable without issue is strong but somewhat irresponsible. A librarian cannot assume that a collection of digitized audiovisual material in one format will be easily mutable another ten, twenty, or fifty years thence. The strongest part of the laissez-faire approach is actually admirable: the most important thing that a librarian can do to a digital file is ensure its security. If technologies arise that accommodate any file format, thereby making it playable by anyone with a computer, it will be more important that the source file be available and uncorrupted. The problems in migration do often overshadow the simple fact that so many digital audiovisual resources are stored on external hard drives or on portable devices such as laptops rather than secure network storage.

The Project

With the three concepts of understanding grasped, it leaves only the necessity for implementation. This is a trial in and of itself, as the acquisition of legacy audiovisual equipment and other attendant technologies can be an exhausting and trying experience. The understanding of users, collections, and products provide more than enough supporting knowledge for a project, though, and can be used to create truly effective delivery mechanisms for information. The costs of acquiring equipment, labor, and expertise will be overshadowed by the resultant interest in a well-planned and well-executed audiovisual digitization effort. This book systematically guides readers from the foundation of a project (or program) to the end product. While many projects and programs do not ever end per se, the continued management of goals and expectations is covered in detail, keeping in mind the major points of users, collections, and products.

Key Points

The three basics of managing digital audiovisual resources are not immutable and can be defined differently among persons in divergent contexts. The most important thing to remember, though, is that users/audiences, collections, and products will always be the highest considerations when embarking upon a digitization effort. Collections will always be the cache from which content is drawn; users will always be involved; and a final product will always be the metric by which the success of a project or program is gauged. In keeping with the trio of concepts discussed here, the next chapter explores the finer points of collection assessment and description, in terms of both media and content. It delves into the differences between analog and digital materials, as well as what separates special and circulating collections, discussing a variety of formats and content types.

What Do You Have?
Evaluating Collections

Knowing Your Collections

Understanding the types of materials in a collection is the first step in the journey toward making that collection accessible and interpretable. Having vast audiovisual resources is meaningless without a thorough understanding of their makeup, as well as an understanding the resources required—technological and otherwise—in realizing their potential. Many collections in small and large libraries alike go unused or at least underutilized because their curators are unaware of their natures and what the real demand is for their use. This is not to say that these curators are lacking but that audiovisual collections are intrinsically difficult to comprehend, describe, and organize, even to the most experienced archivist. In general, very little is understood of how many audiovisual resources truly exist in the collective library environment and even less about why they arrived where they did. There are clear reasons for this mystery, such as the relative newness of audiovisual resources compared to literary; but there are also unclear reasons, as in why the muddy provenance of some collections end up in libraries, with little or no subjective relativity.

This chapter sheds light on the differences between audiovisual resources within a library's circulating collection and those in its special collections. While the objects in the former were once modern formats, they now share more with the legacy materials housed in the latter. This chapter also discusses the inherent differences between materials that are analog and those that are digital. Common formats, physical and digital, are discussed in detail, and recommendations are made for further readings and informative resources. With the information presented in this chapter, an archivist, librarian, or curator should be able to easily identify the nature of a common audiovisual object (analog vs. digital), its type (e.g., VHS vs. U-Matic), its content, how to review it, and its potential usefulness. Finally, this chapter serves as the foundation for the rest of the book, defining the core terms, concepts, and technologies discussed in greater detail in later chapters.

⑨ Special versus Circulating Collections

It is likely that the majority of audiovisual collections earmarked for digitization are those housed in special collections departments. Such objects tend to be historical artifacts, records of events, or the lives of persons, which are not entirely unlike paper correspondence in a manuscript collection. Given the nature of these objects and their general lack of restriction on legal reproduction and distribution, they tend to be easier to digitize and present. The only permission required in digitizing and presenting an oral history record on a media server may be that of the donating agent, although such permission is often predetermined during acquisition. However, circulating collections are likely to be less easy to digitize. Much of the audiovisual content housed in and circulating through a library or library system is licensed for use only by one patron at a time and cannot be duplicated. Objects such as feature films, documentaries, and books on tape are subject to the same copyright laws as any other similar objects found in a retail store. Because of these restrictions, they cannot simply be digitized and streamed. Even if special permission is obtained, there will likely be limitations to use for the digital version. The following two sections—Special Collections and Circulating Collections—go into deeper detail in comparing circulating and special collections and how to approach them.

Special Collections

By their very nature, special collections can house an unchecked variety of materials. Manuscripts, maps, rare books, folios, audiovisual artifacts, and more all make up the ecosystem of a special collection. Their foci can range from history local to the managing institution to collections of national significance acquired serendipitously. Regardless of origin or relative importance, special collections require much more attention, description, and interpretation of their handlers than the objects in a circulating collection. This necessity is due to the complexity, condition, and rarity of a special collection's components, which suffer more from overhandling than the more robust materials in circulating collections. Most significant, though, is that special collections often have limited appeal and are used with greater intensity by fewer persons than common books and DVDs. The letters and photographs of a local political figure or the oral histories of an unknown blues musician are, of course, esoteric and will likely never see as much use as a DVD copy of a well-known film used by a cinema history course. Advances in digital humanities research and the growing appeal of special collections by way of digitization have increased the exposure of special collections making them more accessible and applicable to more than just the most focused researchers.

Among the most interesting artifacts in special collections are audiovisual artifacts, which can include anything from motion picture film to LaserDiscs to DVDs. Regardless of format, what unites these objects is their historical nature. While a book on tape contains information and may be "old," a singular oral history on the same kind of medium has intrinsic value because of its rarity, its author/subject, or both. Digitizing such objects is often the only way to properly preserve them, as the virtual shelf lives of digital objects are considerably longer many physical formats. Other objects are digitized to increase their exposure. Many special collections, audiovisual or otherwise, may be well managed but known to only a select few. The notion that digitizing for preservation and exposure is the ideal platform for a special collection is discussed at greater length in chapter 6.

In the United States, there are some very notable academic and nonacademic special collections with highly advanced audiovisual collections, such as the Archive of Recorded Sound at Stanford University and the Museum of Modern Art's Film Study Center in New York. Either these collections have made points to specialize in audiovisual objects, or, by virtue of geography or serendipity, they have historically been entrusted with curating and preserving such materials. This guide is more concerned with institutions that have small- to medium-sized special audiovisual collections and no history of curation and focused pursuit in this area.

Circulating Collections

What circulating and special audiovisual collections share in format they do not often share in rarity. Circulating audiovisual collections are generally more robust than special ones but tend to be represented more by common titles. For example, a circulating collection may have hundreds—if not thousands—of items, but many other libraries have the exact same titles in their own collections. If uniqueness defines special audiovisual collections, commonness defines circulating. This is not to suggest that circulating audiovisual collections are not worth the effort required to digitize them but that more thought should go into the objects on which a librarian should focus or whether the collection should be approached holistically.

Circulating audiovisual collections can include VHS tapes, CDs, audiocassettes, and DVDs, among other formats. These materials were (or are) acquired much like print materials in a library and run the gamut from educational documentaries to feature films and books on tape. While CDs and DVDs are effectively "digitized," which is to say that they exist as digital media and can easily be transferred to other digital media, VHS tapes and audiocassettes require the same kind of processing as similarly formatted objects in special collections. Unlike special audiovisual collections, circulating ones have typically experienced more use and are likely to be in worse condition. Analog media especially, like VHS tapes, can show signs of wear when replayed, as they have likely been handled and played thousands of times since being acquired. This wear and tear is one of the reasons to consider digitizing circulating audiovisual collections, as they will likely only deteriorate further.

Digitization of circulating collections can also be justified by the "obsolescence factor." It is reasonable to assume that most patrons have the technology necessary to replay DVDs and CDs, but the same cannot be assumed of their ability to view VHS tapes and audiocassettes. Many libraries keep VHS decks on hand to accommodate individuals who need to view a VHS tape, but this mode of access is costlier to patrons (they must always come to the resource) and eventually to the library, as it must maintain one or more VHS decks, which are increasingly becoming harder to find. Furthermore, VHS tapes and their players are less and less familiar to most patrons, a trend that will only continue. Therefore, it is necessary to adapt to current trends rather than force a library's patronage to conform to obsolete tools. Many of the pathways for adaptation available today are discussed in chapter 6.

Finally, given the age of many circulating VHS and audiocassette collections, digitization may be the only path to migration (see textbox 2.1). Many VHS documentaries and books on tape may not be available on newer media such as DVDs, CDs, or file-based

TEXTBOX 2.1.

PROJECT STARTERS: CIRCULATING VHS COLLECTIONS

Description

Digitizing traditional circulating VHS collections is becoming more and more crucial in providing access to functionally obsolete formats. Many useful videos are trapped in obsolescence and have little or no use due to that obsolescence. Converting these VHS tapes to digital formats or even transferring them onto DVD media can breathe life—and longevity—into an aging video collection. The most problematic part of engaging in such a venture is the hurdle of permission: most VHS materials, even though they may be obscure, are likely encumbered by copyright. Even though most such videos cannot be obtained in modern formats, steps must still be made to ensure that permission is obtained or at least that a record of due diligence exists.

Common Sources

- Circulating VHS collections

Common Physical Formats

- VHS videocassettes

Digitization Hurdles

- Permission acquisition
- Copy protection features of VHS tapes
- Labor needed to investigate copyright status
- Copyright-sensitive management of files once online

Circulating VHS Collections

While the benefits of digitizing circulating VHS collections to modernize access are clear, not many universities widely advertise such efforts. Investigating whether a library has a collection of digitized VHS tapes once held in its circulating collection is difficult but not impossible. Check with local libraries, academic or otherwise, to see if they are in the process of digitizing their circulating video collections. Many collections may only be accessible to constituents of a library (e.g., university staff, faculty, and students) and may be held in a password or IP-protected streaming media system.

media. It is wise to contact the producers and distributors of the materials earmarked for possible digitization to determine whether the outdated format in questions is in fact the only one available. That determination, coupled with permission from copyright owners, is usually all the clearance that a librarian needs to begin migrating. The steps in this process are covered in greater detail in chapters 6 and 7.

◎ Formats

To understand collections, special or otherwise, a librarian must first be able to determine the format of an object or objects. It is never usually necessary to have encyclopedic knowledge of every format ever made, but it is important to have a topical understanding of the differences between analog formats and digital and the key materials therein. This section covers the basics of analog and digital audiovisual formats, the most common objects in either category, and how to identify some less common ones. Finally, lists and recommendations are provided for modern resources for identifying audiovisual objects.

Analog versus Digital

There is much literature, in print and on the Internet, that details the many differences between analog and digital objects. For the purposes of this guide, a basic but useful definition is given that should be more than ample for the purposes of most readers. *Analog* and *digital* refer not necessarily to the physical medium but to the signal used to record on the medium (e.g., digital signals can be carried on physical tape). In short,

> *Analog signals:* continuous ranges transferred to a medium as waves or pulses
>
> *Digital signals:* discrete values transferred to a medium as binary values

Analog signals, whether from audio or video inputs, are interpreted by the recording mechanism as waves, pulses, or even some physical features (e.g., vinyl records). It is easiest to think of analog signals as measurable waves of information transferred directly to a medium capable of aligning to those signals. A common metaphor for analog signals is a mercury thermometer, which, while not as precise as a digital thermometer, shows continuous movement of temperature. For example,

- Vinyl records receive information on their surfaces as grooves (or, in the case of antique vinyl, bumps and dips) that modulate (or physically change) during recording.
- VHS tapes receive information on their magnetic surfaces and align to incoming signals.
- Film is exposed to light and captures images in succession.

Digital signals, regardless of the input, are "samples" of binary (1's and 0's) information recorded without regard to range. It is easiest to think of digital signals as chunks of relatively consistent data. Common metaphors for digital signals are light switches, which are either on or off and are measured as such. For example,

- Audio CDs contain binary information represented as microscopic pits that are then translated into sounds.

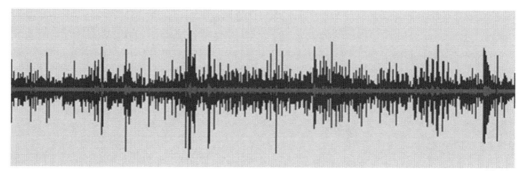

Figure 2.1. Analog Wave.

- Digital videotape has magnetic properties like analog tape but receives binary information rather than wave ranges.

Perhaps the best illustration of the difference between analog and digital signals is the difference between a continuous sound wave, as in an audio editing program (figure 2.1), and that same wave broken up into discrete values, resembling the arrangement of sliders on a graphic equalizer (figure 2.2).

The most important thing to remember about the differences between analog and digital signals is that the latter are far more common than the former in modern applications; the reverse is true with regard to special collections in libraries, as they act as repositories of historic objects. Knowing the complex mathematics behind signal processing is not a prerequisite to being an effective curator or archivist of audiovisual materials. It is important, though, to have a topical understanding of the nature of such objects and how to communicate productively with stakeholders, vendors, and other professionals.

Analog Formats

Analog formats tend to be the most common audiovisual material types found in a special collections department and likely constitute a significant portion of circulating collections. As discussed earlier, such formats are media upon which signals are impressed, written, or, in some cases, carved. The visual and structural variety among analog formats is greater than that of digital ones and can often pose quite a hurdle for librarians and curators, inexperienced or otherwise. Some common formats include

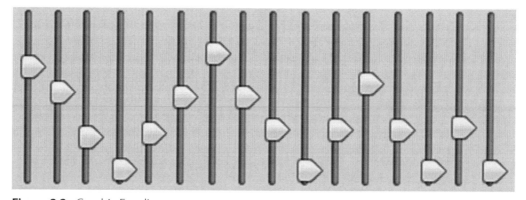

Figure 2.2. Graphic Equalizer.

- Vinyl records
- Reel-to-reel quarter-inch audiotape
- Audiocassettes
- VHS videotapes
- U-Matic videotapes
- Betacam videotapes
- Motion picture film

There are dozens of other formats, but the aforementioned are the most common analog objects found in library collections, special or circulating. Analog formats do not enjoy the same life span as digital ones and are more likely to suffer from decay. Well-maintained videotapes can be replayed for decades, but because of the nature of analog playback, which involves the moving of tape or other media across sensors, recordings will degrade over time. This degradation is inherent in the replay of many analog media and is unavoidable. For example, vinyl records are read by a needle attached to a tone arm that follows the bumps, dips, or grooves of the record and converts them to sound. The action of dragging a needle over pliable vinyl—however advanced the playback system is—results in physical degradation over time.

Other media—such as audiocassettes and videotapes, which "hold" data magnetically—can suffer from natural degradation of their iron oxide coating, which results in poor-quality playback. VHS tapes, audiocassettes, and quarter-inch audiotape are also prone to breakages, as they are dragged through, across, and around a variety of mechanisms that can put stress on them and eventually cause them to snap, curl, or wrinkle. Simple repairs can remedy most of these issues, but some media require the handiwork of a professional. Motion picture film, for example, cannot simply be taped back together like quarter-inch audiotape and must be repaired by professional film restorers.

Even more complex is the repair and preservation of nitrate-based film, which, unlike relatively harmless acetate film, releases nitric acid as it decays and is highly flammable. Nitrate film is not likely to be found in most special collections, but acetate film is and should be handled with great care. As acetate film degrades, it releases acetic acid, which, while not particularly dangerous, exudes a vinegar-like aroma and is a textbook indication of decay, which eventually leads to shrinkage and brittleness.

As is discussed in chapter 5, there is a variety of equipment that a librarian must possess and understand to digitize analog formats. Much of this equipment is difficult to acquire because of its rarity and cost, but some components can be found and purchased with nominal effort and expense and make productive additions to a digitization unit. Most audiovisual digitization vendors possess nearly every necessary piece of equipment required to digitize a variety of formats and can serve a special or circulating collection well. More on the vendor–owner relationship and how to maintain it is discussed in chapter 5.

Common Analog Formats

There are far too many analog formats to discuss in this book, but this section details the appearances, backgrounds, and peculiarities of the most common analog formats. The following format profiles include brief histories, physical descriptions, and images. Note that for the analog videotape formats profiled, a *video cassette recorder* or *VCR* is a generic term that applies to the equipment used to replay and record all videocassette formats.

History and use. VHS tapes are one of the most successful analog audiovisual formats ever manufactured. Introduced in the late 1970s by the Victor Company of Japan (IEEE Global History Network 2012), VHS videotapes (figure 2.3) were the preferred consumer video-recording medium for over two decades and represent an overwhelming portion of the collected analog audiovisual materials in the world. VHS players, or decks, were available to the average consumer by 1978 and permeated the home video market soon after. Though poorer in build and recording quality than its competing format, Sony's Betamax, VHS's low cost and open design quickly became the consumer standard. This dominance in the home video market continued through late 1990s until DVDs (digital video discs) rose to prominence. Identical in size and shape to VHS, Super VHS (S-VHS) videotapes provided better quality playback and fidelity. They were not as successful as VHS videotapes, however, as S-VHS players and tapes were slightly more expensive and the market generally preferred the low cost and acceptable picture quality of VHS.

Description.

Cassette build:

- Cassettes measure 7 3/8 × 4 1/16 × 1 in.
- Hard plastic.
- Flip top protects the tape and can be easily opened by depressing a push-in toggle on the right side of the top edge.

Details:

- Two spaces for labeling on front and bottom.
- Two clear plastic windows showing the tape's reels.
- Inscriptions indicating brand and type.
- Variety of colors, typically black.

Figure 2.3. VHS Cassette.

Medium:

- Magnetic tape ranging in length from 412 feet (60–120 minutes) to 1,427 feet (216–432 minutes).

Container:

- Cardboard slips.
- Plastic snap cases.

Playback. VHS VCRs are capable of recording and replaying VHS tapes but cannot accommodate S-VHS tapes. However, either format can be replayed on and recorded through S-VHS-specific VCRs. It is common to find backward compatibility like this in a variety of VCR devices across many formats.

Betamax

History and use. Betamax (figure 2.4) was developed by Sony and released in the mid-1970s as a consumer-grade recording and playback format. Often referred to simply as "Beta," this tape format and its developers were embroiled in a fierce format competition against VHS, with the latter eventually winning out and taking hold in most world markets (Owen 2008). Betamax tapes were significantly smaller than VHS and exhibited higher-quality recordings. In spite of these two technical advantages, the low manufacturing costs and resultant consumer price of VHS VCRs and tapes were too challenging for Betamax to overcome. Furthermore, given Sony's reluctance to license Betamax in the same way that Victor Company of Japan did VHS, competition was stiff. Betamax tapes may arise from time to time in archives but are almost nonexistent in circulating collections. Betamax was widely used in its day by educational organizations and artists, so if they are discovered, they are likely to contain amateur videos or institutional content.

Figure 2.4. Betamax Cassette.

Description.
Cassette build:

- Cassettes measure 6 1/8 × 3 3/4 × 15/16 in.
- Hard plastic.
- Flip top that protects the tape and can be easily opened by depressing a toggle along the left side of the cassette toward the top edge.

Details:

- Areas for labeling along the bottom front.
- Clear plastic window exposing one reel.
- Small Greek beta character (β) on the upper right of the tape's front or along its left side, depending on the brand.

Medium:

- Magnetic tape, 1/2 in. wide.
- Run time, depending on tape, ranges from thirty minutes to three hundred, though sixty-minute run times are most common.

Container:

- Cardboard slips.
- Plastic snap cases.

Playback. Betamax tapes can be replayed only in Betamax VCRs, which were manufactured by Sony.

Betacam, Betacam SP

History. Betacam (figure 2.5) was released by Sony in 1982 and marketed to the professional audiovisual market. While Betamax was squarely defeated by VHS in the consumer market, Betacam and its in-family successors are still used today by professional videographers in production environments. Similar to Betamax in construction, Betacam captured a much higher-quality recording and became a favorite standard among the television broadcasting industry. Shortly after Betacam was released, a higher-quality version called Betacam SP entered the market and was adopted by television studios and filmmakers as a mastering format. It is also common to find archival footage in Betacam SP, with much of it having been transferred from an older format. Betacam SP tapes and decks are still being produced today in a very limited way.
Description.
Cassette build:

- Handheld recorder cassettes measure 6 1/8 × 3 3/4 × 15/16 in. (identical to Betamax).
- VCR tapes measure 9 5/16 × 5 11/16 × 1 in.

Figure 2.5. Betacam SP Cassettes.

Because of their identical sizes, an archivist should take care not to confuse smaller Betacam or Betacam SP tapes with Betamax—they require completely different VCRs and offer different playback qualities.

Details:

- "Betacam" or "BetacamSP" labels inscribed on the front of each tape.
- Labeling space located on the front and along the bottom.
- The smaller Betacam cassettes reveal only one spool through a transparent plastic window, while the larger tapes reveal both spools on either side of a labeling area.

Medium:

- Magnetic tape, 1/2 in. wide.
- The smaller Betacam family tapes used in handheld video cameras have a run time of 62 minutes, while the larger tapes could hold up to 194 minutes.

Playback. Betacam VCRs are capable of playing only Betacam tapes, but Betacam SP VCRs are capable of playing both formats. Betacam-family VCRs were produced by Sony and Ampex.

U-Matic

History. U-Matic tape (figure 2.6), often referred to simply as *three-quarter-inch tape*, was introduced by Sony in 1971 and is among the first commercially available videocassette formats in North America. It was intended for use by average consumers, but the high cost of manufacturing both the tapes and the VCRs made U-Matic more affordable for professionals and was readily adopted by the television broadcast and other industries (Sony History 2012). Given its newness at the time of its release and its ability to be manipulated by persons without high levels of audiovisual prowess, three-quarter-inch tape was also favored by educational institutions, and many tapes can be found originating from well into the 1980s. U-Matic VCRs and tapes are no longer produced but factor as a particularly large portion of the archival video environment, perhaps second only to VHS. A smaller, higher-quality version called U-Matic SP was released in the mid-1980s.

Figure 2.6. Typical U-Matic Cassette.

Description.
Cassette build:

- Typical cassettes measure 8 5/8 × 5 3/8 × 1 3/16 in.
- Small cassettes measure 7 1/4 × 4 5/8 × 1 3/16 in.

Details:

- Gray, black, or off-white.
- Small red plastic "dot" on back that can be removed to prevent recording.
- Dominant labeling area on front.
- Clear plastic window (or windows) on front revealing one reel or both.

Medium:

- Magnetic tape, 3/4 in.
- Larger tapes have a sixty-minute run time and smaller ones, twenty minutes.

Container:

- Large, flat, roughly textured snap case.
- Large, bulky case with rounded edges and sliding latch.

Playback. U-Matic VCRs can play any variety of U-Matic cassettes regardless of size or generation. However, if a U-Matic tape is played in a U-Matic SP deck, there will be some diminishment in replay quality.

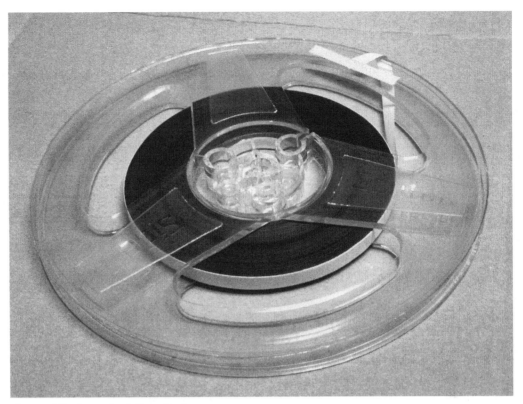

Figure 2.7. Seven-Inch Tape Reel.

Reel-to-Reel Audiotape

History. Used as a far back as the 1930s, reel-to-reel, or quarter-inch, audiotape is a common find among archival audiovisual collections. Reel-to-reel tape (figure 2.7) deserves an entire book on its history and development, but while the reels that hold it and the devices that record and play it have changed over the decades, the tape material itself was rarely improved on. Amateurs, professionals, organizations, governments, and just about any other entity imaginable used reel-to-reel tape. Even the smallest archives often possess dozens of tape reels, containing either the oral histories of individuals or recordings of lectures or radio broadcasts. The format eventually became portable, which enabled thousands of scientists and researchers to bring equipment with them to far-flung locales, spawning countless field recordings of everything from the behaviors of wild animals to oral histories of persons in remote corners of the earth.

Description.
Reel build:

- Plastic or metal, diameter of 7 or 10 in.
- Center hole for mounting on playback device.

Details:

- Various colors, levels of translucence, and textures.
- Tape medium is typically brown or reddish brown.

Medium:

- Magnetic tape, 1/4 in. wide.
- Play time is dependent on length of tape and the speed at which it was recorded (faster speeds = better quality but less total record time): 1,200 to 1,800 feet on 7-in. reels and 2,500 to 3,600 feet on 10-in. reels.

Container:

- Simple, flat cardboard box (most common).
- Plastic snap case (less common).
- All containers likely to be heavily branded by makers' marks, decals, and logos.

Playback. Reel-to-reel tape is recorded on and replayed by a variety of devices with dozens of physical configurations. An archive is most likely to either own or have access to a vertically configured reel-to-reel player from the 1970s or 1980s. Common and reliable player/recorder brands still available in the secondhand market include Otari, Teac, and Sony.

Phonograph Records

History. Phonograph records, more commonly referred to as *records*, are part of a family of sound media dating back to the nineteenth century. While there are dozens of types of records, an archivist in the average archive is most likely to encounter either vinyl LP (long play; figure 2.8) or EP (extended play) records—or, in some cases, much older 78-rpm records, which were made from shellac, a substance much harder, heavier, and less flexible than vinyl (Yale University Libraries 2012). It is rare to find nonmusic recordings on vinyl or shellac, as disc media were more difficult to record on than reel-to-reel tape. For the purposes of distribution, however, discs were more practical, and localized reproductions of educational or institutional recordings on vinyl are not rare. Vinyl records are still produced today to distribute music recordings but do not experience the same level of acceptance and use as CDs or digital music files.

Description.

Record details:

- Vinyl colors vary; the most common is black.
- Twelve-inch variety has small hole in center; 7-in. type has much larger one, requiring an adapter during playback.
- Labels are typically around center hole.
- Weight and flexibility vary by size and age; older vinyl records are thicker and heavier while younger ones are noticeably floppier.

Medium:

- Vinyl, sound modulation inscribed.
- 7- to 12-in. diameter.

Container:

- Cardboard sleeve, sometimes with interior paper protector.

Figure 2.8. LP Phonograph Record.

Playback. Record players, or phonographs, are still manufactured and are far more advanced than they were just twenty years ago. Modern players can play vinyl LPs (33 1/3 rpm), EPs (45 rpm), and records (78 rpm), as well as shellac phonograph discs. Even if an archive owns an antique gramophone or phonograph, it is advised that he or she not use it to replay shellac or vinyl records of any speed, as the heavy tone arms and steel needles can damage and eventually destroy recordings. Modern electric turntables employ light, balanced tone arms that hold platinum alloy or diamond needles, which are less likely to damage or wear out recordings.

Audiocassettes

History. Audiocassettes, or compact cassettes, are one of history's most successful audio-recording mediums (figure 2.9). Introduced in the 1960s, audiocassettes gradually grew in popularity, peaking in the 1980s with the wide consumer adoption of portable cassette players, most notable of which was Sony's Walkman. Much like VHS tapes, audiocassettes were inexpensive, both to produce and to purchase, and could be easily wielded by amateur audiophiles. Audiocassettes were supplanted by compact discs (CDs) in the 1990s but still exist as a niche product. A smaller variation called a *microcassette* is also fairly common and was used primarily for recording voice via miniature handheld field recorders. While much smaller than typical cassettes, microcassettes have roughly the same length and record times as their larger cousins, a quality achieved through the utilization of thinner tape. Archivists are likely to have more audiocassettes than they

Figure 2.9. Typical Audiocassette Tape.

know what to do with, as they were widely used by researchers and a variety of academic professionals to record oral histories, interviews, and lectures.

Description.
Cassette build:

- Cassettes are 4 × 2 1/2 × 3/16 in.
- Microcassettes are 2 × 1 1/2 in.
- Two sprockets.
- Clear plastic or opaque.

Cassette details:

- Labeling space on either side.
- Medium exposed along bottom.
- Various colors and textures.

Medium:

- Magnetic tape, 3.81 mm wide (microcassette and regular cassette).
- Total lengths vary from 433 feet to more than 450 feet.
- Record time is typically thirty minutes per side for either size.

Container:

- Hinged plastic case, usually transparent with labeling inserts.
- Small plastic snap case.

Playback. Audiocassette players are still produced today and are fairly easy to locate and acquire. Older devices are widely available on the secondhand market and, depending on brand, very reliable. Players produced today are usually professional grade and have at least two cassette decks, auto-reverse (which automatically plays a tape's opposite side once the other has completed playing), and noise reduction technology, which enhances playback and recording. An archivist or a librarian may encounter a variety of devices, including the aforementioned professional decks but also once-ubiquitous devices, such as Sony's Walkman personal player, tape decks combined with CD players, and handheld audiocassette recorders. Microcassette tapes can be played in a variety of miniature handheld field players/recorders but cannot be played in standard audiocassette decks.

Motion Picture Film

History. Of the media detailed in this chapter, motion picture film has the longest and most complex history. Developed in the late nineteenth century by Eastman Kodak, flexible motion picture film stock made the film industry possible by standardizing the material used to record and deliver motion pictures (Kodak 2012). Before Eastman Kodak's breakthrough in flexible film stock, early experimental devices used glass, paper, and other materials to attempt to record and project film. Early film stock and the photosensitive emulsion that captures images were based on cellulose nitrate, a highly flammable material that often caught fire during projection and is very unstable (Health and Safety Executive 2010). Most nitrate film stock in the world has decomposed on its own or was destroyed by accident or intention, but some is still kept in climate-controlled archives around the world. In the 1930s, nitrate film was replaced by stock based on acetate, which is far more stable. By the middle of the twentieth century, polyester stock rose to prominence and is still in use today. An archivist may encounter a variety of sizes, or gauges, of film, but the most common are

- 35 mm (feature motion pictures),
- 16 mm (documentary features, stock footage, educational films), and
- 8 mm (amateur films and stock footage).

Depending on the archive or library, 16 mm is the most likely to be encountered, as it was commonly employed by educational institutions to capture events/lectures or produce instructional films (figure 2.10).

Description.
Reel build:

- Metal.
- 3- to 16-in. diameter.
- Thickness dependent on film gauge.

Reel details:

- Reels are a variety of colors.
- Center holes for mounting on projectors.

Figure 2.10. Sixteen-Millimeter Film on Reel. *Courtesy of Wikipedia User: Holger.Ellgaard.*

Medium:

- Emulsion on nitrate, acetate, or polyester.
- Gauge/width of 35, 16, or 8 mm (various other sizes exist, though are rare).
- Film length and running time examples: 35-mm reel = 1,000 feet and 11 minutes, 16-mm reel = 800 feet and 29 minutes, 8-mm reel = 300 feet and 21 minutes.

Reel containers:

- Metal canisters, various colors and textures.

Playback. Film is replayed through a device called a *projector*, which shines light through each frame on a film as it passes by an aperture, the enlargement of which is projected on a screen or flat vertical surface. Projectors are difficult to come by today unless significant investment is made in a professional-grade device. Inexpensive finds of 16-mm projectors are not rare in the secondhand and online markets, but the effort to gather such equipment is risky and time-consuming. Most likely a specialized vendor already has the necessary equipment and is capable of converting film to digital formats. Of all the formats detailed in this chapter, film is easily the most difficult to work with and is best left to specialists.

Physical Digital Formats

Physical digital media include, for example, digital audiotape, digital videotape, and CDs and DVDs. These formats are physically extant and tangible but do not contain data in the same way that analog formats do. A musical performance is recorded on a vinyl record as a series of modulated grooves that correspond to the actual modulations of the performance; the same performance recorded on a CD—or mastered on digital tape and transferred to CD—is simply a series of binary values (1's and 0's) that are interpreted by some other mechanism as sounds. In some ways, a CD and a vinyl record are similar: both are round, and both hold data on one or both sides as pits or grooves. The difference is that the grooves on a record are literally shaped like the sounds they hold, while the pits in a CD correspond to binary digits that note values in the sounds they hold.

The following physical formats are the most common and might be encountered in a library or archive.

Optical Disc Media: CDs, DVDs, and LaserDiscs

History. Optical formats are one of the most common and successful mediums for the delivery of sound, video, and software, many flavors of which are still in use today. While used in different ways and, in the case of LaserDiscs, manufactured in different sizes, all optical media function in the same way: they are written upon with a laser that alters the surface of the disc to create pits and lands (i.e., low spots and even spots). Changes among the sizes of the pits and the distance between them (lands) are interpreted by another laser as audiovisual signals or other data during playback. The three optical disc formats most likely to be encountered by a librarian or an archivist are CDs, DVDs, and LaserDiscs:

CDs: Introduced in the early 1980s, audio compact discs (or CDs) were not commercially successful until the 1990s, when players became less expensive and more portable (figure 2.11). CDs exhibit superior sound quality than that of their onetime competitor, audiocassettes, and quickly became the quintessential music medium of the 1990s. Still produced and sold today, CDs have fallen in popularity to file-based

Figure 2.11. Compact Disc.

Figure 2.12. DVD.

music formats such as MP3 and MP4, which are commonly downloaded directly from sources on the Internet rather than physical stores. The same technology was used for many years as a software delivery medium, a use also transferred to the Internet and more advanced media, such as DVDs and Blu-ray discs.

DVDs: Introduced in the mid-1990s, DVDs rose to prominence in the twenty-first century as the most popular medium for viewing motion pictures (figure 2.12). DVDs were successful in supplanting the preferred consumer movie medium and led to the latter format's quick demise in the first decade of the twenty-first century. DVDs are still produced today, though they have lost ground to the popular high-definition Blu-ray format, as well as file-based video.

LaserDisc: Introduced in the late 1970s, LaserDiscs (figure 2.13) were intended to be the successor to cassette tape formats in the delivery of video. However, due to the high cost of both the players and the discs, LaserDisc never had much success in North America. Many thousands of motion picture titles were produced on the format, though, and LaserDisc saw wide use in educational institutions, often being used to present photographic slide shows or high-quality instructional videos.

Description.
Disc build:

- Circular.
- Center hole for mounting within playback mechanism.
- Flexible polymer.

Figure 2.13. LaserDisc. *Courtesy of Wikipedia User: Kevin586.*

Disc details:

- Semitranslucent.
- Blank or labeled on surface of one side.

Medium:

- Optical.
- 4.7-in. diameter (CDs, DVDs).
- 11.81-in. diameter (LaserDiscs).

Container:

- Hinged plastic cases referred to as a "jewel cases," typically with label inserts (CDs).
- Large opaque plastic snap cases with label inserts (DVDs).
- Cardboard sleeves with plastic protectors (LaserDiscs).

Playback. CD players come in a variety of shapes and sizes and can still be purchased at common retail outlets around the world. CDs can be played in almost any optical disc-playing device, including a CD-ROM drive on a computer or a DVD or Blu-ray player. DVDs can be played in either a DVD-ROM drive on a computer or DVD or Blu-ray player; they cannot be played in a CD player or CD-ROM drive. LaserDiscs, mostly due to their nearly foot-long diameter, can be played only in LaserDisc players, which are increasingly difficult to find, even in the secondhand market.

DV and Digital8 Tape

History. While it seems odd given what has been covered thus far, digital media can be recorded onto magnetic tape. Developed in the mid-1990s, DV (digital video) was created to replace other, more cumbersome analog tape formats for the purposes of professional and amateur recording. *DV* can refer to either the cassette-enclosed tape format (figure 2.14) or the file-based format; the latter is more relevant today, but DV tapes are still produced and are common finds in library archives. They come in a variety of sizes and run times, including MiniDV, DVCPRO, and DVCAM. Digital8 is a digital version of the analog 8-mm videotape format, Hi8, which was popular for home recording in the 1990s. Digital8 and DV tapes have nearly identical tape and quality, and both use the same digital codec (DV). The main differences are the cassette sizes and the transport mechanisms, which are not interchangeable with DV tape players and recorders.

Description.

Case build (tape formats):

- MiniDV: 2 9/16 × 1 7/8 × 7/16 in.
- DVCPRO: 4 7/8 × 3 × 9/164 7/8 × 3 × 9/16 in.
- DVCAM: 4 7/8 × 3 × 9/16 in.
- Digital8: 3 11/16 × 2 3/8 × 9/16 in.

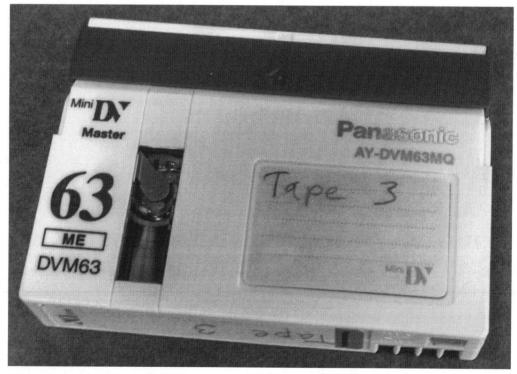

Figure 2.14. MiniDV Tape Cassette.

- Plastic.
- Clear tape windows.

Details:

- Variety of colors, typically gray or black.
- Variety of textures and label configurations.

Medium:

- Magnetic tape, 1/4 in. wide.
- Lengths vary by cassette size.

Container:

- Hinged plastic cases with label inserts.
- Hard plastic snap cases.

Playback. DV is still a relevant format, so playback decks and handheld recorders are being produced. DV tapes, especially MiniDVs, are usually played back through a video camera rather than a standalone playback deck, though such devices exist. Digital8 has fallen out of favor, but cameras and playback decks are still being produced in fairly limited quantities.

File-Based Digital Formats

File-based formats are not linked to a physical medium like their tape-based digital relatives and really only share their binary nature and the occasional terminological crossover. File-based media formats are those that were likely never recorded on a physical medium, digital or otherwise, and are intangible. Granted, these formats exist on a physical storage medium (e.g., solid-state drive, hard disk drive) but tend to be kept as immaterial data rather than moved to a physical delivery medium, such as a CD or digital tape. Moreover, file-based digital formats number in the hundreds, and their use is the subject of much debate by the sound and audiovisual engineering community. Formats in this category are standards for containing what are called *codecs* (compression/decompression), which are simple programs employed in the compression and interpretation of audiovisual signals. These format-codec combinations are used to store archival copies of audiovisual streams or deliver them to users.

Generally speaking, a person will encounter or create two kinds of digital media files:

Compressed files: video or audio that has been compressed from its original size to a smaller, more manageable size for use in file delivery. The process of compression usually leads to some amount of data loss and degradation in media quality. Some modern codecs are capable of compressing raw media without any appreciable loss in data, referred to as *lossless compression.*

Uncompressed files: video or audio that was captured from an input source, such as a microphone, camera, or analog playback machine, and is contained without being compressed. Files in this category are typically very large and can be unwieldy. For example, during capture, one minute of analog video translates to one gigabyte of raw digital video.

Whether files are compressed, losslessly compressed, or uncompressed, it is important to understand the difference between a format and a codec when dealing with file-based media:

Container format: the vessel in which audiovisual streams—and the codec that compresses and decompresses them—are stored. The format also determines how the audiovisual streams are played and by what program.

Codec: a portmanteau of "compression" and "decompression." A codec is a series of algorithms used to decode, compress, and, during playback, decompress audiovisual streams.

It is easiest to think of a container format as a file's extension (e.g., .avi, .mp3, .ogg); this is often the case, as many formats dictate extensions, which in turn dictate the program that a computer uses to open certain media files. A codec, however, is like the blueprint within that container, which instructs the media player how to decompress audiovisual streams and at what quality and rate.

There are hundreds of container formats and codecs, but this chapter details only a handful of the most common combinations and where they are most often encountered. For example, the Library of Congress maintains a highly detailed and oft-updated list of digital file formats (multimedia and data) and their sustainability factors. The site http://www.digitalpreservation.gov/formats is a collaborative U.S. government effort led by the National Digital Information Infrastructure and Preservation Program.

Common Formats, Codecs, and Configurations: Video and Multimedia

The following video and multimedia formats, codecs, and configurations are common finds among library archives, collections, and institutional records.

MP4 and H.264/AAC

Background. MPEG-4 Part 14 (MP4) is one of the most common multimedia container formats used today. It was developed by the Motion Picture Experts Group (MPEG) to contain codecs and data streams like any other container format but with a preference for H.264 (MPEG-4 Part 10) video and Advanced Audio Coding (AAC) audio. These data streams are among the most advanced and have become the preferred combination for delivery of audiovisual information across the Internet. H.264 is currently the video compression standard for Sony's popular Blu-ray disc technology, and AAC—the effective successor to MP3 audio—is, among other credits, the preferred codec for compressing music files delivered via Apple's iTunes store. MP4 with H.264 and AAC is widely used in web-based media streaming systems, as this format and codecs have been widely adopted by web browsers as standard delivery streams. The MP4 container format is very similar to the older QuickTime format (MOV) developed by Apple. While MP4 and QuickTime share many similarities, the former takes advantage of a variety of MPEG specifications that make it unique.

Common file extensions.

- .mp4
- .m4v
- .m4a (audio streams)

Common occurrences and uses.

- Delivery of online video or audio files
- Delivery of streaming video through media streaming systems
- Output from popular video-editing software, such as Apple's Final Cut and Sony's Vegas programs
- Files from student art projects
- Institutional repositories

MPEG-2

Background. MPEG-2 is a common container format typically holding two transport streams: one video and one audio. It has been used for many years as the basic format for delivering television signals, either over airwaves or through a hard connection. MPEG-2 is also the container format used to carry audiovisual information on a DVD and is often referred to as *DVD video*. The codecs used within MPEG-2 files vary, with the video stream often being H.262 or MPEG-2 Part 2 and with the audio being MPEG-1 Audio Layer III (MP3) or MPEG-1 Audio Layer II (MP2). MPEG-2 has largely been eclipsed by MP4 and other more advanced codec-container combinations that allow for more audio and video streams, as well as more complex metadata. Given its popularity via DVDs and acceptance as a broadcast standard, MPEG-2 is a common occurrence in archives and special collections and will remain so for many years.

Common file extensions.

- .mpeg
- .mpg
- .mp2 (audio)
- .mp3 (audio)
- .ts

Common occurrences.

- DVD video and audio
- Broadcast archives
- Library archives

DV File

Background. DV (digital video) is a common container of uncompressed or losslessly compressed audiovisual streams. DV was developed in the 1990s as a concurrent file-based format to tape-based media such as DV tape and is still in use today. Many handheld DV cameras record directly into a DV file, which can then be manipulated in a video-editing program. A librarian is likely to encounter DV if he or she is entrusted with preserving content from a series of digital tapes (which are typically captured as DV) or the contents of a DV camera. DV is sometimes described as an "initial state" format, which indicates its raw nature. From this raw file, a librarian or technician would make an archival copy that is playable by more systems and programs than those associated with video-editing suites.

Common file extensions.

- .dv (most common)
- .dif (less common)

Common occurrences and uses.

- DV recording
- Video editing
- Student art projects
- Institutional videos

QuickTime

Background. QuickTime File Format (MOV) is part of a much larger series of formats, codecs, and algorithms, all under the QuickTime framework. Apple developed this framework as its default multimedia distribution and playback system, which is still in use today. Within this framework, MOV is the most well known and widely accepted container and is often used as an archival format or for delivery. Apple video-editing products, such as Final Cut and iMovie, provide the option of exporting to MOV, which can contain a variety of codecs but most often holds H.264 and AAC.

Common file extensions.

- .mov
- .qt

Common occurrences and uses.

- Export from Apple video-editing products
- Archival file format for DV

Audio Video Interleave

Background. Audio Video Interleave (AVI) is perhaps the most well-known—and certainly one of the oldest—container formats. Microsoft developed AVI in the early 1990s for use with its Windows Media Player, as well as for distribution over the Internet. AVI is old and has been surpassed in terms of sophistication by other containers, such as MOV and MP4, but given its widespread use and proliferation in the early days of the World Wide Web, it still enjoys widespread use. It is often used as an end-state archival container for raw video but is also capable of containing compressed audiovisual signals.

Common file extensions. AVI is always represented by the ".avi" extension.

Common occurrences and uses.

- DV delivery
- Archival videos
- Video editor export format

Windows Media Video

Background. Windows Media Video (WMV) is a widely used multimedia compression codec and container developed by Microsoft. It was intended for use with Windows Media Player but is playable in a variety of modern players. It is most often paired with Windows Media Audio (WMA) for distribution of video created by Microsoft video-editing programs.

Common file extensions. WMV is typically only presented with a ".wmv" file extension.

Common occurrences and uses.

- Video editor output format
- Video-streaming systems
- Video clips
- DV distribution

Common Format-Codec Configurations: Audio

The following audio formats, codecs, and configurations are common finds among library archives, collections, and institutional records.

MP3

Background. Established as a standard for distributing compressed audio, MP3 is easily the most successful digital audio format in history. In the mid-1990s, MP3 became the de facto delivery vehicle for digital music and, for the most part, is still an accepted and usable format in almost all portable digital music players. While MP3's compression algorithm and audio fidelity are not as advanced as MP4's, its small size, portability, and universal acceptance are unparalleled. Many common recording devices, such as digital field recorders, automatically save audio input as MP3, thus making it a near certainty that an archivist or a librarian will encounter this format at some point in his or her career.

Common file extension. MP3 files typically present with only the ".mp3" extension.

Common occurrences and uses.

- Digital music
- Delivery of audiobooks, either over the Internet or on CD media
- Oral history files
- Student music projects
- Institutional repositories
- Faculty lectures

Waveform Audio File Format

Background. Waveform Audio File Format (WAV) is a highly successful audio container format that has been in use since the early 1990s. Microsoft developed the format to contain audio for use in its Windows Media Player and other Windows- or DOS-specific system players, but it can contain nearly any audio codec. WAV files are most commonly used to hold uncompressed audio, such as like Linear Pulse Code Modulation audio for archival storage or delivery, via either the Internet or public airwaves. WAV files are simplistic and versatile, and although many other container formats are far more advanced (e.g., FLAC), WAV still enjoys wide use and universal acceptance.

Common file extensions.

- .wav
- .wave

Common occurrences and uses.

- Audio or music delivery over broadcast airwaves
- Archival audio
- Sound clips

Audio Interchange File Format

Background. Developed by Apple in the late 1980s, Audio Interchange File Format (AIFF) files are de facto raw audio containers for Apple-based systems. In that regard, AIFF files are similar to Microsoft's WAVs. However, perhaps due to the early proliferation of Windows-based systems, AIFF has not enjoyed the same wide recognition. Most modern software audiovisual players are capable of handling AIFF files, though, and these files are still used by Apple users in audio production and to store archival audio.

Common file extensions.

- .aiff
- .aif
- .aifc (compressed)

Common occurrences and uses.

- Archival audio
- Audio editing

Windows Media Audio

Background. WMA is to audio what WMV is to multimedia and video. Similar to WMV in that it is both a container and codec, WMA was designed as a competitor to the popular MP3 format but did not enjoy as a wide a distribution or adoption. WMA files are most often encountered by librarians when interacting with audio collections that were created in a Microsoft-based audio editor.

Common file extensions. WMA typically presents with only the ".wma" extension.

Common occurrences and uses.

- Audio-editing program export format
- Sound clips
- Digital audio distribution

RealAudio

Background. RealNetworks developed RealAudio files in the mid-1990s as a variable-size audio format that utilized a variety of codecs. The most significant use of RealAudio was through its creator's successful RealPlayer, a streaming audio program that helped popularize Internet-based radio stations. RealAudio is not as widely used as it was in the 1990s and early twenty-first century, but examples can be found within almost any audiovisual collection. A librarian encountering a RealAudio file will find that said file is either indeed an audio file or, as is sometimes the case, simply a shortcut to an audio file on the Internet, in which case it would be played through RealPlayer.

Common file extensions.

- .ra
- .ram (links to RealPlayer)

CD Audio and DVD Video

Both CD and DVD media can contain most any kind of data, and it is not uncommon for a person to encounter a disc with its capacity filled with audio or video files. These discs and their files are fairly easy to work with, as the contents are obvious. Audio CDs and video DVDs, however, are not always so transparent. In some cases, a librarian may need to extract data from a professionally created music CD or video from a DVD, and upon inspection in a computer, either medium will display files not quite as well known as MP3s and MPEG-2s. DVDs, especially those with visual menus, utilize a container format called Video Object (VOB), which contains video and audio. In most cases, it is necessary to only copy these files directly to a computer and change the file extensions from .vob to .mpg, as VOB files are really just combined MPEG-2 video and MPEG audio streams.

Music CDs, or any audio CD that was professionally created, will appear to contain Compact Disc Audio (CDA) files. CDA files, unlike the VOBs in a DVD, cannot simply be copied to a computer and converted to something more recognizable. CDA is a stand-in format created by the CD drivers in a Windows-based computer. Because tracks on a CD are arranged more like those on a phonograph record, the CDA files simply act as references to data rather than the data themselves. To extract the actual tracks from a CD, they must be "ripped" by a program that converts the CD audio to a usable format.

⊚ Further Resources

There are hundreds of reputable and rich resources available to librarians and archivists regarding audiovisual technologies and formats. The following resources are reputable and can be consulted and compared when delving deeper into the world of digital audiovisual preservation, digitization, and recognition:

Audio and Video Carriers, by Training for Audiovisual Preservation in Europe (2008), http://www.tape-online.net/docs/audio_and_video_carriers.pdf. This guide on audio and video formats (carriers) is exhaustive and details the history behind core formats, their preservation, and maintenance.

Conservation OnLine, by the Foundation of the American Institute for Conservation (2013), http://cool.conservation-us.org/. This website, while poorly organized, is a valuable clearinghouse in audiovisual preservation and collection information.

Guidelines on the Production and Preservation of Digital Audio Objects, by the International Association of Sound and Audiovisual Archives (2009), http://www.iasa-web.org/tc04/audio-preservation. This guide on preserving digital audio is an invaluable resource from one of the world's most respected professional organizations.

Survey Instrument for Audio and Moving Image Collections, by Columbia University Libraries (2013), http://library.columbia.edu/services/preservation/audiosurvey.html. This tool is useful for individuals—professionals and amateurs alike—to assess and catalog the various materials in an audiovisual collection. It does not explain or detail the intricacies of formats directly but provides unique cataloging specifications for each supported format and is helpful in reinforcing learned concepts.

Sustainability of Digital Formats Planning for Library of Congress, by National Digital Information Infrastructure and Preservation Program (2013), http://www.digitalpreservation.gov/formats/index.shtml. This catalog of digital audio and video formats is detailed and exhaustive. It provides technical information on formats and codecs, as well as how to assess the sustainability of each one.

VideoPreservation Website, by the National Center for Preservation Technology and Training and the Bay Area Video Coalition (2013), http://videopreservation.conservation-us.org/index.html. This website is a clearinghouse for audiovisual preservation and identification resources assembled by the center and is an excellent springboard to finding authoritative sources.

Videotape Identification and Assessment Guide, by the Texas Commission on the Arts (2004), http://www.arts.texas.gov/wp-content/uploads/2012/04/video.pdf. This guide is among the most referred-to and well-presented resources on identifying videotape formats. It includes photographs, technical information, and further resources.

Key Points

This chapter explores a variety of analog and digital formats, but it only scratches the surface of a very broad field that no single resource can comprehensively discuss. A basic understanding, though, is extremely valuable in the world of audiovisual technology and digitization, as it allows a person to establish a comfortable rapport with his or her materials. From this firm jumping-off point, a librarian can explore more advanced topics in audiovisual formats and, more important, have the foundational knowledge necessary to discuss these technologies intelligently with vendors and persons in allied fields.

Furthermore, when the kinds of materials in an archive or collection are understood, a librarian will be able to make sound decisions on what his or her institution is capable of supporting. For example, if a librarian is presented with a donor's collection of 16-mm films, the contents of which are subjectively relevant to the institution's mission, he or she will be able to make a better decision about whether those films can be properly cared for and curated. It may be the case, in this situation, that despite the subject matter, the curation of the films is simply too expensive an undertaking. Also, understanding the various and sundry audiovisual materials in a current collection and the limits of their usability will make curation and the decision to digitize much easier. The key points of this chapter are as follows:

- Basic understanding of differences between analog and digital formats is necessary in curating and managing all audiovisual materials.

- Even cursory audiovisual knowledge will help librarians speak intelligently with vendors and colleagues in the field.
- It is less important to be an expert in audiovisual technology than it is to know the correct resources—and persons—to consult.
- Circulating and special collections, while possibly overlapping, are different and should be treated differently when planning a digitization program.
- A firm foundation in the basics of audiovisual formats will help librarians better understand their holdings and make more informed decisions about collecting and planning.

Perhaps what is most important to remember from this chapter is the difference between analog and digital formats, as well as special and circulating collections. Knowing that processes applied to one format or collection may not necessarily be transferable to another is a valuable lesson. This is a lesson with which librarians and archivists are likely already familiar, as the curation and presentation of print materials and other physical, nonaudiovisual objects are part of their regular duties and the same prohibition of assumption exists therein. This speaks directly to the importance of deciding the correct kinds of materials to collect based on previous behaviors; librarians and archivists often steward collections that they did not pursue, and many important factors have to be considered when deciding whether to build on historical audiovisual collections.

References

Health and Safety Executive. 2010. "The Dangers of Cellulose Nitrate Film." http://www.hse.gov.uk/pubns/indg469.pdf.

IEEE Global History Network. 2012. "VHS Standard." http://www.ieeeghn.org/wiki/index.php/VHS_Standard.

Kodak. 2012. "Milestones-Chronology." http://www.kodak.com/ek/US/en/Our_Company/History_of_Kodak/Milestones_-_chronology/1878-1929.htm.

Owen, David. 2008. "The Betamax vs. VHS Format War." Mediacollege.com. http://www.mediacollege.com/video/format/compare/betamax-vhs.html.

Sony History. 2012. "The Video Cassette Tape." Sony.net. http://www.sony.net/SonyInfo/CorporateInfo/History/SonyHistory/2-01.html.

Yale University Libraries. 2012. "The History of 78 rpm Recordings." http://www.library.yale.edu/cataloging/music/historyof78rpms.htm.

CHAPTER 3

Evaluating Collections: Picking a Direction and Developing Collections

LIBRARY COLLECTIONS DO NOT FORM IN VACUUMS and are highly dependent on their geographic contexts, institutional histories, and simple serendipity. Special collections in particular are prone to context and serendipity, as they tend to focus on a few subjects relevant to the library's region, but they are also common repositories for miscellany. Many special collections librarians and archivists find themselves with collections that are a mix of local relevance and wildly divergent subjects. For example, a library in Florida that specializes in local history can be home to objects such as Gutenberg Bibles and ancient Chinese pottery. Audiovisual collections within any area of a library are no different: whether bequeathed from local collectors with esoteric interests or transferred from circulation to archives because of obsolescence, audiovisual materials are subject to the same acquisition norms and phenomena.

This chapter explores strategies and tactics that archivists or administrators can wield to identify the scope of their collections, as well as how to proceed in complementing those collections, digitizing them, or determining whether procession is necessary or feasible. It may be that a library has significant audiovisual holdings through some acquisition but little or no resources to exploit them or preserve them. For a variety of reasons, a library may not have the subjectival expertise necessary to truly engage and promote a significant audiovisual collection. The tactics discussed in this chapter will prepare readers to survey their current collections and make informed determinations of what they and their administrators are capable of in terms of curation and how to take the next step. The strategies discussed are more concerned with library-wide policies that dictate—based on the outcomes of less expansive tactical decisions—how the library deals with audiovisual collections or whether it chooses to avoid them entirely, deferring to better equipped or simply more interested institutions.

⑥ Tactics: Evaluating Current Audiovisual Holdings

Many library special collections do not have a collecting arm dedicated solely to audiovisual or multimedia objects. It is more likely that a special collections department inadvertently has audiovisual objects, ones that came with manuscript collections or as part of larger, more diverse acquisitions. In such cases, audiovisual objects stored alongside paper manuscripts are either unknown (unless the collection has been fully processed and described) or known but perhaps not being given due consideration. While it is certainly acceptable to store materials by subject and not medium, researchers are occasionally interested in media independent of context. For example, a professor or student might want access to all videos, films, or audio recordings of a generic subject, but the desired materials may be spread across a dozen collections and difficult to extract individually. Even if audiovisual objects are stored by medium, they may not be playable unless the library has the necessary equipment. These concerns are part of understanding the short-term tactical approach that an archivist must wield to do what is best for the materials and the library.

Basic Questions to Ask

It is important to ask the correct questions when deciding how to approach a collection so that the answers, whatever they may be, are appropriate, informative, and relevant. The following questions should be posed when deciding how to evaluate and manage an audiovisual collection in the short term:

- How many audiovisual objects are in the collection?
- What subject areas are represented?
- How often are the objects used?
- Should the audiovisual materials be separated from other objects?
- What is the overall condition of the materials?
- Should the materials be digitized?

For the sake of illustration, each question is applied to a hypothetical institution, Ivan State University Library, which has a medium-sized collection of VHS tapes, audiocassettes, and reel-to-reel tapes spread across a variety of manuscript collections representing several subjects.

How Many Audiovisual Objects Are in the Collection?

Though simplistic and perhaps obvious, knowing the precise number of tapes, videocassettes, and films that exist in a collection is the foundational question in which all other questions should be anchored. If a collection possesses only a few VHS tapes and a single reel of 16-mm film, it will be far easier to answer every other question that follows; a collection rife with videocassettes and reel-to-reel tape will pose significant challenges and new questions that are unnecessary to ask in other cases. The best way to answer this question is by referring to container lists and finding aids, which accompany individual collections in special collections, and by simply taking a physical survey of every collection's containers when there are gaps in available data. In the case of circulating collections, it would be easiest to restrict a database search to item types.

Ivan State University Library, because of its small special collections staff, has not had the resources to fully describe and process its many manuscript collections, but because of past experiences and patron interactions, the library's archivists were aware that they had at least a few dozen VHS tapes and dozens of audiocassettes interspersed throughout their holdings. To get a precise count, the archivists and student assistants at Ivan State methodically sifted through each collection's containers and counted all audiovisual items. When they finished, the archivists discovered that they had a collection of 147 audiocassettes across three collections, 54 VHS tapes across two collections, and 20 reel-to-reel tapes in one collection yet to be described or processed.

What Subject Areas Are Represented?

Once the total number of objects is known, it is necessary to ascertain the subject areas represented and whether there is any overlap among media. Even if a special collections department prefers separation of audiovisual media from its acquired manuscript collections, this question still needs to be asked, as the subjects may vary wildly. The process of identifying subjects for individual items across a variety of collections is not always direct; it may be necessary to view the materials to determine their subjects, but given limitations in access to legacy audiovisual playback devices, this may not be possible. However, archivists are trained to make educated guesses about the subject of any object given its age, context, and the collection through which it was acquired. It is important to note that labels do not always reveal the true contents of any objects, let alone audiovisual ones, which are particularly prone to relabeling or, in many cases, loss of labeling.

The archivists at Ivan State University Library discovered 147 standard audiocassettes across three institutional collections, which were only partially processed. Given the documentation accompanying the collections, as well as the other materials within, the archivists were able to determine that most, if not all, the audiocassettes they found contained oral histories and interviews of Ivan State alumni, professors, and prominent visitors conducted by Ivan State University historians. Because the library had access to a cassette deck, the archivists were able to briefly listen to each tape and confirm their contents.

Ivan State's archivists were also able to identify the subject areas covered by the fifty-four VHS tapes they found. Among the tapes, twenty-two were discovered to be part of an institutional collection pertaining to the Ivan State University College of Veterinary Medicine. A brief viewing of each tape in the department's VCR revealed that the tapes to be a mix of recorded classroom lectures and institutionally created educational videos intended for the general public. The remaining thirty-two tapes were discovered among the archives of Ivan State's College of Journalism and contained recordings of student-created news broadcasts.

The archivists of Ivan State University Library were not so lucky when it came to the twenty reel-to-reel tapes they discovered within the manuscript collection of a famous local author. While the tapes were dated during the lifetime of the famous author, they had no further information to offer. Because of the sometimes-disconnected nature of personal manuscript collections, the archivists knew not to assume too much about the contents of the tapes beyond their connection the collection's donor.

How Often Are the Audiovisual Objects Used?

A core activity in maintaining any collection is the gathering of usage statistics. At their most simple, these statistics will reflect the number of uses for each object or the collections containing them. More advanced statistics might take into account the origin of the user and whether that user, or others, repeated visits to use the same materials. Documented evidence of a collection's usage can assist in its promotion and help librarians and archivists make strong cases for funding.

The archivists at Ivan State University kept copious records related to patron interactions and item usage. Because of this record keeping, which was digital, the archivists were able to determine that the journalism and veterinary medicine VHS tapes were used regularly, some titles as much as five times a month.

Should the Audiovisual Objects Be Separated?

Depending on the total number of items and their particularity among the entirety of special collections, it may be necessary to hold audiovisual items in a separate container or space. Doing so will make their study and use by patrons easier to facilitate, as they will not be in dozens of locations around an archive. Granted, for some collections, removing and relocating individual items from a named collection is not desirable, as a special collection may have a robust and sophisticated item-finding system in place that would fail were items to be individuated. The decision to separate should be based on a combination of size, use, and specialization: if an audiovisual collection is very large (more than five hundred items) and is used often (metrics vary from library to library) and if the library actively collects audiovisual materials as a rule, then separation is ideal.

The archivists at Ivan State decided to separate out some objects but not all. As the oral histories on audiocassette all pertained to the lives and times of Ivan State alumni and persons of note and the collections in which they were kept were general institutional collections, the Ivan State archivists decided to create a virtual collection of oral histories while still referencing their origins and provenance. The reel-to-reel tapes, because of their closeness to their collection and their uncertain contents, were not separated out. However, because of frequent requests for the VHS tapes in the College of Journalism and College of Veterinary Medicine collections, the Ivan State archivists opted for separation.

What Is the Overall Condition of the Materials?

Audiovisual materials in a special collection are sometimes in worse condition than paper-based objects. This has little to do with negligence on the part of librarians and archivists and more to do with the focus of collections, which tends to be paper oriented. Videocassette tapes, reel-to-reel tapes, and films are all subject to decay and mishandling in much the same ways as papers and photographic prints. The damaging factors tend to be the same: overabundances of heat and humidity and improper storage can cause significant damage to audiovisual materials. It is good for every archivist and librarian in the position to manage such collections to understand a little bit about the proper care and handling of audiovisual materials. One of the best and most concise resources in this field is the Library of Congress's Collections Care website, specifically the section dealing with audiovisual materials, which can be accessed at http://www.loc.gov/preservation/care/record.html. A collection manager need not know every facet of the science behind audiovisual deterioration and decay, but she or he must be aware of the signs and symptoms exhibited by materials in distress. For film, the National Film Preservation Foundations offers a well-prepared guide on identifying decay in various types of film materials. A free electronic version of this guide can be accessed at http://www.filmpreservation.org/preservation-basics/the-film-preservation-guide. The overall condition of a collection can be a determining factor in its digitization and whether its managers wish to relocate it to an institution better equipped to deal with such materials.

The archivists at Ivan State Library found no apparent signs of wear or significant indications of damage to the oral history audiocassettes, which were surprisingly free of disruption when replayed. The reel-to-reel tapes, because of Ivan State's lack of a player, could not be listened to, to ascertain any detectable damage. It was noted that some of the tapes appeared to be wrinkled and that several reels appeared to have been improperly spliced. Finally, the Ivan State archivists found that the VHS tapes of the College of Journalism and the College of Veterinary Medicine showed several common signs of wear. Using the web-based *A/V Artifact Atlas*, which can be accessed at http://preservation.bavc.org/artifactatlas/index.php/A/V_Artifact_Atlas, the Ivan State archivists were able to determine that the videotapes exhibited tape crease and dropout, both indications of high use.

Should the Audiovisual Materials Be Digitized?

Deciding whether to digitize audiovisual materials is similar to the decisions inherent in digitizing most other materials. Cost of digitization, local technological resources and expertise, and patron needs are all factors that an archivist or librarian should consider when embarking on any digitization effort. What separates audiovisual digitization from other projects are the technological hurdles: optical scanners, cameras, and other devices used to capture images from paper materials are very common in the library world and can be acquired along a sliding scale of price and complexity. Audiovisual digitization, however, is reliant on a mix of modern equipage and obsolete and hard-to-find playback devices, such as Betamax players and reel-to-reel decks. Luckily, there are dozens of digitization vendors that specialize in audiovisual digitization and work with libraries and archives to capture content from obsolete formats.

Technological hurdles aside, archivists should consider what is to be done with the videos and audios once they are digitized. Digital repositories are commonplace and typically have a complement of digitized audiovisual resources to local or broad public consumption. However, as is sometimes the case with either copyright-restricted materials or special collections for which digitization is proscribed, digitization can simply be considered a preservative measure. Digital files can be kept in perpetuity with minimal risk of loss, and if restrictions on display lapse, they will be ready for immediate consumption.

The archivists at Ivan State University Library decided that, given the high use and apparent wear of their VHS tapes, digitization for preservation and access would be prudent. As the College of Journalism and College of Veterinary Medicine are both part of the university, the tapes were determined to be free of restriction, and, given their frequent usage, wider online access would reduce stress in the physical objects and broaden their reach. However, due to the apparent fragility of the reel-to-reel tapes and the unknown nature of their contents, the Ivan State archivists thought it best to have the tapes digitized for preservation only, at least until the contents could be reviewed and any possible restrictions revealed. As for the oral history audiocassettes, the Ivan State archivists decided that their fair condition did not beg preservative measures, but their medium amount of use might be increased were they to be digitized simply for access purposes. However, since the oral histories were recorded before such things as web-based access were a consideration, permission from the interviewees would have to be attained before the files could be made publicly available.

Implication of Answers

When the aforementioned questions are answered, it will be much easier for an archivist to make better-informed recommendations to his or her institution's administrators on how to proceed with larger, more involved strategies for collection development. If the outcome is a positive one wherein an archive's collections are retained and promoted, it could prove to be the catalyst for the acquisition of more audiovisual materials. However, if it is determined that the archive's collections are minimal and irrelevant to the overall mission of the library, then a precedent will be set allowing archivists to safely resist further audiovisual acquisitions. In the example of Ivan State University Library, where a mix of formats and subjects were discovered, it is likely that the archivists and librarians there would be apt to proceed with the continued curation and development of current collections and the acquisition of new materials (see textbox 3.1).

Strategies: Building a Collection Development Policy

Tactics are helpful in determining short-term activities and assessing immediate needs. Strategies are broader and more comprehensive, taking into account short- and long-term approaches to collections. When the questions of immediate need are answered, it is prudent to then look at the goals, mission, and identity of a collection. Many special collections are composed of wildly disparate subject areas, the comprising collections acquired serendipitously or without much direction. In such cases, strategies are created on the basis of the subject or materials most well represented by a collection, or they are devised on the basis of concrete determination irrespective of collections. Other special collections and archives are highly focused and carry one or two themes particularly well. Strategies in focused archives are generally easier to establish, as there is likely already a specific development policy that directs collection development.

The following determinants will be key in choosing the direction in which special audiovisual collections are to be taken. Situations vary from institution to institution, so all determinants discussed may not be applicable to every case. These determinants

TEXTBOX 3.1.

PROJECT STARTERS: DOCUMENTING YOUR ARCHIVE

Description

While most librarians and archivists do a magnificent job protecting resources and providing meaningful access to collections, they do not always tend so diligently to their own promotion. It is not unheard of for local television news entities, either professional ones or those administered by students, to do exposés of entire archives or specific collections therein. But rather than rely on external parties, it should be the responsibility of the library to promote and document its own resources. Such an effort could be looked on as a metadocumentation of the myriad collections held within an archive or special collection. Video documentaries could be made showcasing individual collections, featuring on-camera interviews with the archivists, subject specialists, and staff that made the collections usable. Once assembled, these videos could serve as promotional material or simply a cross-referential way of keeping track of the why, how, and when of each collection. Eventually, these videos would themselves attain some archival significance.

Common Sources/Collaborators

If there are no individuals at your library who have expertise in videography or marketing, it would be wise to approach entities that do. If money is a concern and professional (external) videographers are not within budget, decision makers should pursue a homegrown source. For example, many universities and colleges maintain an academic technology or videography division that supports the directorial and audiovisual efforts of faculty and staff. If such divisions exist at your institution, they might be able to assist in production of metadocumentaries at a much lower cost than that of any external professional.

Common Physical and Digital Formats

Naturally, all content produced for an archive documentary project should be digitized (or born digital).

Project Hurdles

- Cost to hire external videographers or co-opt local staff
- Time needed to effectively plan and produce content
- Planning for promotion and for whom

Circulating VHS Collections

Any libraries that maintain a regularly updated program to document their archives and collections may not make content readily available. The best method for figuring out which institutions do maintain such materials is simply to ask. Also, scouring libraries' YouTube or Vimeo pages will likely yield positive results.

assume that all tactical questions have been answered and that an archivist or librarian understands the boundaries and breadth of his or her collections.

Determinants for Setting a Collection's Course

Determinants are the factors by which an archivist gauges the essence of a collection and its relationship to the institution of which it is part. Once identified, these determinants can be congealed to inform decisions about a collection's direction and will assist in crafting a collection development policy. In summary, the determinants are

- Collection size
- Collection rarity
- Collection scope
- Academic support
- Technological support
- Financial dedication

Collection Size

The total number of audiovisual items will determine the overall need for establishing a direction. As covered by the first tactical question, size typically translates to immediacy: large collections require more attention sooner; small collections generally require less attention, unless rarity is a factor. If it is a factor (discussed next), then even a small collection will have the clout that it needs to progress. In this context, progression means that a collection will be wholly supported and hopefully built on.

Collection Rarity

Collection rarity is a determinant whether a collection is large or small, but in the case of the latter, it could be the deciding factor in whether to pursue a strategy regardless of all other factors. Rarity is assigned to the content of the object (singular audio interview with a famous person), the format (rare 78-rpm gramophone record), or both. Whether something is rare or not can be decided by archivists, librarians, or appraisers. It is not likely that an entire collection is composed such items, but some pieces are certainly rarer than others.

Collection Scope

Collection scope refers to the subjects, themes, and foci of a collection or collections. Some collections are highly focused and may contain materials from only one or two major themes with a few subthemes. For example, a special collection might be known for collecting original audio recordings, interviews, and ephemera related to local or regional musicians, but the same collection may have little or no resources on literary history. Other collections lack any kind of focus and are a mélange of subjects that are interrelated or have no ties whatsoever. Aside from collection size, scope is likely to be the most important determinant in the development strategy of a collection. The subject matters and themes covered by a special collection or archive can lend to the total identity of a library and its institution, especially if those themes are well represented, preserved, and supported.

Academic Support

Librarians and archivists have specializations and areas of expertise, but they alone cannot fully support an archive or special collection. The determinant of academic support refers to subject expertise of local teaching faculty, subject librarians, and other researchers who can offer guidance in how to proceed with collection development. When looking at a specific collection, a librarian must determine whether its subject matter can be properly addressed and interpreted so that users will benefit as much as possible. For example, if a library somehow possessed a medium-sized collection of avant-garde short films on VHS, would they continue to build such a collection if the university of which they are a part had no film or media studies program? Moreover, collecting materials in line with an institution's strengths (e.g., Latin American history) will enhance the usability and grasp of the materials and those who seek them.

Technological Support

The technological know-how and equipment at a library's disposal will determine how its collections are used. This determinant is not limited to digitization, as even a library with little or no appropriate audiovisual equipment or expertise on hand can employ the services of a qualified vendor. Technological support also comes from IT (information technology) departments, including programmers, web developers, and graphic designers. These experts and the digital repository technology they support can determine whether a library digitizes just for preservation or for preservation and access, as well as the level of that access. It cannot be assumed that audiovisual resources can just be posted on a library's website or on YouTube and access has been granted users; materials have to be curated and contextualized (by subject experts or librarians), especially when visibility of those materials increases. Technologists are crucial in facilitating the practical processes inherent in digital curation.

Financial Dedication

A dedicated source of funding is essential to maintaining a strategy, whatever that might be. While libraries rarely purchase special audiovisual collections (or any special collections), each collection costs money to maintain, describe, and curate. The following are common costs associated with audiovisual collections that will have an impact on strategic determinations:

- Student labor for assistance in collection processing
- Equipment purchases for reviewing materials or digitization
- Purchase of digital repository or audiovisual streaming software for access
- Repair costs for damaged media and playback devices
- Archival storage costs for raw (uncompressed) digital video files
- Secure storage for physical items

Grants can be useful in funding a project in the short term and are often how libraries acquire some kinds of specialized equipment, but a program has to have the full support of its library to enjoy long-term success. When funding is low or nonexistent, materials cannot be effectively digitized, curated, and promoted, and the users of those materials—researchers, students, and faculty—will suffer as a result.

Crafting a Collection Development Policy

Once an archivist and her or his team have assigned values to the previously discussed determinants, the creation of a holistic strategy can begin. Such an activity rarely happens in a vacuum or as the result of one person's input, but it is usually an assemblage of different experts' decisions as well as the output of some other administrative oversight mechanisms. These pieces form a document, often referred to as a collection development policy, which dictates the decisions that a collecting body makes when developing and curating its holdings. It is wise to allow for some flexibility, as circumstances change over time and what worked during one administration in one time span may not work in another. Flexibility can also work to the library's and archivist's advantage: allowing for variances in a strategy, or leeway, can permit an organization to gather materials and collections in slightly different directions or alongside nontraditional partners that would otherwise have gone untapped.

The form and content of the document will vary from institution to institution and can cover an entire special collection, circulating collection, or simply one area of a single collection. The breadth of a collection development policy will likely be dependent on the previously discussed determinants and the focus and direction of a library. Some good examples of real-world policies are found here:

- Special Collections and University Archives of Vanderbilt University, http://www.library.vanderbilt.edu/speccol/policies/collectiondevelopment.shtml
- Texas Collection and Archives of Baylor University, http://www.baylor.edu/lib/texas/index.php?id=38700
- Arizona State Library, Archives, and Public Records, http://www.azlibrary.gov/cdt/slrspec.aspx

See the sample outline provided (textbox 3.2), which forms the structure of a collection development policy that could be applied to any collection, not just audiovisual ones. Each section is annotated with an explanation.

TEXTBOX 3.2.

SAMPLE OUTLINE OF COLLECTION DEVELOPMENT POLICY

1. Table of Contents
2. Executive Summary: This should include the institution's mission statement or some form of organizational directive relating to the purpose of the library, as well as a summary of what the document will cover.
3. Department Description: This should detail the structure of the department in which the collections being addressed are held and managed.
4. Goals: This section should relate how the collection, whatever it may comprise, is intended to progress. This section need not be overly specific.
5. Audience: This section's intent is to define the individuals and groups at whom the collection is aimed. This can be one of the most flexible and open parts of the policy, as the more groups are considered, the more leeway an archivist has when assembling a project.

---

a. Faculty
b. Graduate students
c. Local researchers
6. Scope: This section should relate the established current breadth of the collection or collections across subject areas. This could be one of the trickiest sections to write, as it can be misinterpreted as items that a library collects rather than what it already owns. A note should be included that differentiates between current holdings and plans for expansion and inclusion.
   a. Institutional history
   b. Oral histories
   c. Local authors
7. Collection Narrative: This section should describe in detail the current holdings of the library's collections. In the case of an audiovisual collection, this should include an overview of each significant collection and examples of the kinds of formats therein.
   a. Ivan State University Institutional Video Collection: a collection of VHS cassette tapes showing the history of several colleges at Ivan State University, including the College of Journalism and the College of Veterinary Medicine.
   b. Ivan State University Oral History Collection: a collection of audiocassette tapes containing interviews with noted faculty, staff, and graduates of Ivan State University conducted by volunteers from the university's public history program.
8. Collecting Criteria: This is the most crucial section of the document and will serve as the rule set to which archivists and administrators refer when deciding whether to acquire new collections or add items to existing ones. It can be a limiting feature if written too strictly; thus, it should be devised with a certain amount of flexibility to allow for interpretation. These criteria should have administrative and subjectival heft, which is to say that they should clearly relate the practicalities of accepting and refusing collections based on finances and relative interest.
   a. All new collections require a signed deed of gift.
   b. All new acquisitions should be in a condition maintainable by current staff.
   c. New collections should be related directly or peripherally to current collection narrative.
   d. All future acquisitions should be accompanied by financial support.
9. Collecting Priorities: This section should detail the current collecting priorities of a library. It is not reasonable to assume that all collections can be pursued equally, so the ones with the most potential should be highlighted and given priority. The success of these collections may allow for the progression of smaller, lower-priority collections at a later date.

It is one thing to define a collection by answering determined questions and using those answers to populate a collection development policy, but the successful application of such a document can be much more difficult. There is certainly a temptation to stray wildly from the confines of a set of guidelines, almost as much as there is to adhere to it with extreme strictness. There must be a balance between adherence and deviation, but identifying the weights on this balance can be challenging. The priorities of any library or collecting body can change from month to month depending on staffing, finances, and administrative behaviors. To complicate things even more, libraries do not exist in vacuums and may have the seemingly overwhelming task of applying a policy to an already established collection that runs counter to current needs and trends. For example, a collection may have been stocked over time with truly random materials with a very loose connection to one another and the institution's mission, and the creation of a new plan (or a first plan) might not leave room for expansion of current holdings. It is wise to include a mix of subject experts, administrators, and external advisors in the process of crafting this document.

◎ Digitization

The next document or series of documents in an archivist's arsenal should be specific to digitization, which can be either holistic or collection specific. Digitization plans can certainly be included in a larger collection development policy, but some archivists might prefer separating strict collecting from digitization, as the latter does not always assume the former: many special or circulating collections can never be digitized and promoted publicly. Regardless of their context, digitization documents are where an archivist can salvage old themes and collections that might no longer be part of current collecting priorities. Digitization, where appropriate and legal, can act as a stimulant for inactive collections and stalled projects, providing them greater exposure and opportunities for enhancement. The next chapter, "Planning for Digitization," guides archivists through the steps of planning for a digitization project by detailing the process of selecting items and securing digitization permission and funding.

◎ Key Points

Assessing and evaluating a collection involves more than just a simple survey and assignation of total value; it encompasses aspects of leadership, determination of audience, budgeting, and policy creation.

The key points of evaluation and developing collections are as follows:

- Ask basic questions, such as how many subjects are represented? what are the conditions of the objects? and should said objects be digitized at all? These will help in the creation of a general idea of where a collection stands and how it can be developed.
- Establish a strategy by addressing determinants such as funding, academic support, and technological wherewithal. These determinants will act as borders for an eventual development policy.
- Create a comprehensive collection development and management policy that can act as a guide—not a commandment—to responsible collecting. Be specific enough to satisfy funding and technological barriers, but be general enough to allow for flexibility in development.

These concepts and tasks, alongside dozens of others, cannot be accomplished unless a holistic plan is in place and followed. Without a plan or some semblance of direction, it is easy to drift among projects or even just ideas without accomplishing anything concrete. That said, it is important to avoid sheer rigidity at the expense of creativity and flexibility. As is the case in many endeavors, balance is key.

Planning for Digitization

PLANNING FOR DIGITIZATION is rarely a simple task. Each project comes with its own set of unique requirements and challenges that must be planned for individually. Policies can be written that cover the general governance of how plans are conceived, what the outcomes of project should be, and how resources are directed toward that project, but rarely are such policies ever capable of expressing specific plans. Case-by-case planning is necessary to the success—or measurable failure—of a project. A solid plan does not account for every eventuality, nor does it necessarily prevent a project's failure, but it helps establish boundaries, which keep a project from becoming unwieldy.

An archivist must make several considerations when planning a project, and a thorough understanding of these considerations will go a long way in increasing the chances of success. Failure, however, is not intrinsically destructive. Even well-planned and well-executed projects encounter insurmountable hurdles that could not have been accounted for. Some fail because the plan was not as precise as it should have been, but even in such a scenario, project managers can look back at the failing, the part of the plan with which it was associated, and make a better determination of how to resolve the issue.

Chapter 4 is concerned with general project feasibility, which can be broken down into several parts. Project feasibility can be determined by funding sources, which might have a bearing on the direction of a project, especially if a grant is involved, which comes with its own set of constraints and goals. Opportunities for collaboration are also explored, as a project plan can be easier to implement when interested external participants are involved. Finally, since many digitization projects, especially audiovisual ones, are subject to some amount of copyright clearance, planning for and around copyright is discussed. Copyright can be project ending, as either a postdigitization mistake or a pre-digitization hurdle; thus, it must be handled carefully and considered in every project.

General Project Feasibility

Given the moving target that is project planning, this book cannot take into account all the factors that determine feasibility. However, it does cover the most common factors and how they might affect a project, positively or negatively. Basically, these factors are as follows:

- Technological requirements
- Personnel requirements
- Cost

These factors are explored from a high level, then related to a specific scenario using the hypothetical Ivan State University Library and its archivists.

Above technology, personnel, and cost hangs the idea of project size, which refers to the scope of the digitization effort, how many individual objects will be digitized, and any associated content goals—whether the digitized videos will be uploaded to a public repository, for example. It is incorrect to assume that a large or complex project is necessarily one wherein many hundreds of items are being digitized: a project with a few dozen items, including their promotion, documentation, and presentation, can be just as time-consuming. If the overall consumption of time, number of project stages, and expected outcomes outweigh a team's resources, then the project is not feasible.

Technology

A project's technological requirements are dictated by the media to be digitized (e.g., VHS tapes), as well as the project's overall goals. For example, although an archivist may know to use the services of a vendor to digitize a collection of quarter-inch audiotape, she or he must also consider the technologies required to host, promote, and preserve the resultant digital files. A technological hurdle or a lack of technology is not in and of itself a project stopper. If the collection is deemed crucial and part of an institution's mission, technologies can almost always be purchased. Requirements might include the following:

- Digitization equipment
- Software
- Digital asset management system
- Servers for storage
- Digital preservation product

Technologies such as these are often applicable to a variety of materials and projects and, if purchased, can prove useful for many years.

Personnel

While having the proper technologies or access to them is important, personnel requirements must be fulfilled to wield those technologies. Many large or well-funded institutions are able to hire ad hoc personnel for specific projects, or they have robust-enough collections to warrant permanent professionals. Administrators of other institutions may find it easier—and less expensive—to shift personnel as needed. If a project is deemed worthy by some metric, the temporary shift of a professional from one project to another is acceptable. Another consideration that a person must make when selecting personnel is how to determine qualifications relevant to the task or whether such a determination is needed. A professional audiovisual technician may not be necessary for a project whose requirements and plan do not dictate that level of attention. Part of a plan, in that case, might be to spend some time training a team member with general knowledge in technologies and audiovisual equipment in the specifics of a project.

Team members might also be drawn from other departments and wielded through differential workload. For example, digitization of audiovisual materials usually requires some level of cataloging support, even if the items in question were cataloged at some point previously. A cataloger involved in a digitization project will likely be a tangential participant, playing his or her part only when called on but never considered a dedicated project fixture. Some other personnel might include

- Information technologists
- Web designers
- Programmers
- Collection development librarians
- Curators

Given the dependence that libraries and archives have on competent professionals, as well as the cost associated with hiring and shifting individuals, personnel and personnel assignment will likely consume the largest portion of any plan. If adequate personnel cannot be assembled, a project might not be feasible.

Cost

The previous factors can be congealed by cost, which is usually the overarching metric by which institutions determine feasibility. Digitization equipment costs money, as does personnel, and in some cases total cost, despite a project's appropriateness or alignment, can stall an effort because of insufficient funding. Establishments can offset costs, however. For example, if an archive already has the necessary digitization equipment and personnel for a project, costs will be lower than if those requirements need fulfillment. A tangible cost—which is to say, a cost that begs equipment and new personnel—is relatively easy to calculate. Intangible costs, however, are not as easily managed. Such costs come from shifting labor or resources (not money) from one project or unit to another, which can incur losses. For example, if a cataloger is pulled from a project on which she or he is working to address metadata issues in another, there could be a cascade of lost time and effort not easily stopped. Time, like money, can be calculated as a discrete cost but is more difficult to accurately assess, as circumstances can change without notice.

Ivan State University Library Scenario

The archivists and librarians at the Ivan State University Library special collection department decided to assess the feasibility of a digitization project involving recorded oral histories (see textbox 4.1). The interviews, recorded on standard audiocassettes, were conducted by Ivan State University volunteers with noted Ivan State faculty. These tapes, which numbered 147 and were in three separate collections, were selected for digitization because of the university's growing public history program, which depends on the conduction of hundreds of oral history sessions every year. Since the oral histories held in the Ivan State Special Collections Department existed before the prevalence of this public history program, librarians, archivists, and professors thought it prudent to build an archive starting with the university's first interviews. Because of special collections' dedicated funding and the project's modest scope, costs were calculated to fall within the boundaries of the department's budget line, and no exterior monetary sources were pursued.

The total project scope includes several components that were determined to be essential in supporting the public history program:

- Digitization for preservation
- New metadata (cataloging)
- Hosting on a publicly accessible digital repository
- Project website
- Promotion through university-specific social media

Components are sometimes change or dropped, so the archivists at Ivan State do not specify the full extent of each component, leaving room for interpretation. Essentially, the expected outcome is a publicly accessible collection of digitized oral histories to which more such files can be added.

Although the Ivan State Special Collections Department did have an audiocassette deck, it did not own any equipment necessary to connect the player to a computer to digitize the tapes. Its options were as follows:

- Purchase equipment and digitize in house
- Send tapes to a vendor

Because the project team was not confident in its abilities to faithfully assemble a workspace for digitizing audiocassettes, nor was it prepared to assume that future needs might justify such an investment, it decided to use the services of a competent audiovisual digitization vendor. The dilemma of whether to digitize in house or use a vendor is discussed at length in chapter 5.

With the digitization covered, the Ivan State archivists realized that they would need to ensure the long-term storage and hosting of the oral histories. Already leveraging a hosted digital repository with built-in preservation tools, the archivists felt confident that their technology needs were fulfilled.

Personnel needs can always be difficult to assess and materialize. While a project can require x number of persons from within an institution, actually getting those persons assembled, accounting for their time, and doing so without compromising other projects is a difficult task. Aside from their professional contributions to the project, the Ivan State archivists determined objectives for the following personnel:

PROJECT STARTERS: ORAL HISTORIES

Description

Oral histories are personal or corporate historical records, usually in the form of one-on-one interviews between historians or volunteers and persons of note. Most such histories were recorded on an audio-only medium (e.g., half-inch reel-to-reel or audiocassettes), but some were recorded in an audiovisual medium (e.g., VHS). In either case oral or audiovisual histories are important links to ancestry and the lives of persons who experienced key historical events.

Common Sources

- University oral history programs
- University journalism departments
- Prominent local individuals—architects, writers, entertainers, politicians
- Local citizens—military veterans, business owners, American Indian tribal leaders

Common Physical Formats

- Quarter-inch audiotape
- VHS videocassettes
- Standard audiocassettes
- Micro audiocassettes

Digitization Hurdles

- Sound quality due to poor recording conditions
- Permission to publicly host files
- Transcription

Oral History Projects

- Samuel Proctor Oral History Program Digital Collection, University of Florida Libraries, http://www.ufdc.ufl.edu/oral
- Collaborative Digitization Project, Western History and Genealogy Collection, Denver Public Library, http://history.denverlibrary.org/research/oral_histories.html
- Oral History Project of the Vietnam Archive, Vietnam Center and Archive, Texas Tech University, http://www.vietnam.ttu.edu/oralhistory/
- Oakland Chinatown Oral History Project, Oakland Asian Cultural Center, http://memorymap.oacc.cc

Cataloger—to create original metadata

Web designer and developer—to create project promotional site

Technician—to upload audio files and metadata to digital repository

Marketing professional—to assist in plan to promote collections

Ivan State University Library was lucky to have a fully staffed IT unit with two web developers and one designer, as well as a fully staffed cataloging department. A metadata specialist in electronic resources was tapped to take on the task of creating original metadata for each of the 147 oral histories, a job that was estimated to take eighty hours and could be completed in less than a month.

The design of the promotional website, with the assistance of one designer and one developer, was slated to be completed in four weeks with some breathing room, as the IT team was already saddled with a few other projects. A part-time student assistant, who was already working in special collections, was reassigned to assist in loading the audio files and associated metadata to the digital repository, as well as assisting in posting updates on the project website. Finally, with all other personnel in place, the Ivan State archivists tasked the library's marketing professional with planning a modest social media campaign directed at key departments and student groups around campus, as well as interested external parties.

Opportunities for Collaboration

Before embarking on any digitization project, a team should consider any and all appropriate opportunities for collaboration. These opportunities can include anything from partnering with a neighboring institution with similar interests and goals to collaborating with a professor who will use the project as part of one of his or her courses. Such collaboration engenders a sense of community between libraries and the people they serve. It also helps lend credence to a project—for example, having support from an architecture school and its faculty during a digitization project in which rare design and architectural history tomes are involved. Experts like that will not only lend credibility to a project (especially if it is grant funded) but simply enhance the final product.

Opportunities may not always be so apparent, but many will in fact be the catalysts for a project, rather than an addendum. University faculty and librarians often have the same missions and interests, but they are not always aware of these crossovers. It is wise to build relationships with key members of the academic community so that the free exchange of ideas among librarians, administrators, and knowledge creators is often and, ideally, expected. An often-overlooked avenue for collaboration is integration of a collection with university-level coursework. The following concept details the importance of such a venture and offers an example of how it can be done well.

Integrating with Coursework

The chief responsibility of academic libraries is the facilitation of information retrieval and interpretation. Inherent in this responsibility is pedagogy, or the science of education. Without libraries, educators, especially at the postsecondary level, cannot effectively teach their students. With the rise of self-directed information retrieval tools, libraries are struggling to remain relevant, and integration with coursework is one of the best ways to do so. While the traditional relationship between librarian and patron is one-way, course integration reinvigorates the pedagogical role of information professionals, allowing them to form a didactic relationship with their charges.

Essentially, coursework integration consists of a preformed partnership between a library unit and an academic department (e.g., archives and biology department) whereby students in certain courses are required to make use of that library unit's resources in person or remotely. This resource can include only a very specific resource, like a masterful reprint of a Gutenberg bible, or can extend to the contents of an entire manuscript collection. The requirement can be that students in a course have to work with the library's archivist to study the history of the book by using primary resources and studying marquee examples.

The most difficult part of this process is usually not in the creation of course criteria or lesson plans but in actually getting commitments from faculty. Many professors and instructors are more than willing to require of their students usage of specific library resources, but not every teacher can modify his or her lesson plans to include a crucial library/archive study module. Postsecondary institutions' policies vary, but most academic courses and accompanying plans need to be approved by departments or even higher-level administrators. While approval is not in and of itself a difficult process, courses are often planned many semesters in advance, and alterations can be laborious. In any case, the potential issues should never be a deterrent to building bridges.

An audiovisual digitization project is a good opportunity to begin a relationship between an archive and either an academic department or an individual faculty member. While planning permanent or semipermanent course integration with a library unit can be a semester-long project, introducing a single assignment or learning exercise into an already-extant course can be a far simpler arrangement and a good way to test an idea. If the project is a success and the participating professor deems it useful to her or his course's vitality, then greater strides can be made toward a long-term partnership.

At the University of Florida in Gainesville, associate professor of English Terry Harpold engaged in just such a relationship with the George A. Smathers Libraries. In the fall of 2007 and 2008, Professor Harpold, working with archivists and librarians from the Department of Special and Area Studies at the university's library, made regular visits to the rare books collection, preservation department, and Digital Library Center a part of his course Interdisciplinary Topics in Literature: Technologies of the Book (Harpold 2007). The goal of the course is related in the course introduction from Professor Harpold's syllabus:

> A review of the 2,000-year evolution of the form of the book most familiar to modern readers—the codex (folded sheets stitched into quires, bound into volumes)—and the changes in reading and writing practices that accompanied its evolution. We will investigate formal, typographic, and mechanical-material traditions of the book, and methods of storing, sorting, selecting, and preserving printed and digital texts. Course fieldtrips will include visits to UF's Special and Area Studies Collections, the George A. Smathers Library's Preservation Department, and the Digital Library Center. (Harpold 2007)

Part of the course was to investigate the history and forms of books, but simply discussing these topics in class was not sufficient: Professor Harpold worked with the university's library to set up field trips and integrated coursework so that his students could experience firsthand the subject matter of the course. While the library did not use Professor Harpold's course as a tie-in to a specific project, the relationship is an excellent example of the general promotion of direct didactic use between a professor and an academic library's collections. If the relationship proved successful and rewarding, it is likelier for partnerships to be implied rather than explicit, at which point the idea of course integration is less an "idea" and more a given.

Cross-Institutional Collaboration

Working alongside outside entities on digitization projects is desirable for several reasons, the most obvious of which is the deflation or distribution of cost. More important than cost, however, is the robustness that collaboration can offer a project otherwise unattainable through a unilateral effort. Where one institution has a specific collection it wishes to digitize, another may have better subject experts that can enrich the end product with interpretation and context. Collaborations also foster long-lasting relationships that will likely be rewarding and productive well beyond the scope of a single project. Granting agencies tend to look fondly on collaborative efforts, which enjoy a level of success and exposure not always shared by projects with little dispensation for outreach. While a collaborative effort in and of itself is not a way to guarantee a grant—nor should it ever be wielded as such (genuine collaboration is paramount)—it can strengthen a proposal that is naturally conducive to cross-institutional efforts.

The University of Florida and Flagler College collaborated on a project between 2010 and 2012 to digitize and preserve hundreds of rare and effectively inaccessible architectural drawings by famed American designers John Carrere and Thomas Hastings. The drawings were discovered in a boiler room at Flagler College in St. Augustine, Florida, and they detailed the design of the Hotel Ponce de Leon and Flagler Memorial Presbyterian Church. The University of Florida kept the drawings for safekeeping in 2005, but it was not until 2010 that a Flagler College professor was awarded a prestigious Saving America's Treasures grant to repair, preserve, and digitize the drawings. The grant awardee saw this as an opportunity to include the University of Florida, which had the technological resources and personnel to take on a two-year digitization project. The project was a resounding success, due in large part to the cooperation between two academic institutions with differing resources but identical goals: preserving and distributing inaccessible historical objects. For more information on the project, the University of Florida maintains a project blog at http://flaglerdrawings.wordpress.com.

Other Opportunities

There are dozens of other ways that a project team can enrich its project by collaborating with others. Adding internships to a project proposal is a good way to include students and experts that may otherwise not be included. Interns tend to have a vested interest in certain subjects and may prove to be more useful than average short-term assistants. For example, were an archivist to embark on a project to preserve and digitize dozens of audiovisual resources from a local journalism program, including interns from that program's current crop of students would be a good way to get contemporary perspectives on the objects and might prove a valuable, long-term inroad with that program.

Sometimes simply collaborating with a single professor or subject expert can be all that is required to enrich a project. Working alongside a literature professor to add context and perspective to the digitization of a collection of taped interviews with a noted local author can help propel a project from simple digitization to knowledge creation. Furthermore, evidence of success with one professor or group of interns will go a long way in proving the effectiveness of an archive and its staff. This evidence will likely make it easier for other projects to succeed.

⊚ Copyright Issues

Project success and feasibility are not always dependent on entirely controllable factors, sometimes hinging on matters of law and luck. As with any digitization project, copyright and usage permission plays a major role in understanding the scope and feasibility of a project, perhaps being the most major factor after general feasibility. If an object—book, videotape, photograph—is to be digitized and publicly displayed, permission must be granted by someone or something. Even if it seems like something is "in the clear," it never hurts to prove due diligence by asking any and all possible copyright holders of an object whether their intellectual property can be digitized and displayed. Yet, if an archivist or librarian wrongly assumes entitlement, the consequences can be project ending or, at the very least, will reflect poorly on the professionalism of the project team and the entire library, especially if the project is high profile or grant funded.

The core of copyright lies in the assumption that every instance of reuse of some property or another mandates permission. It is the librarian's responsibility to either acquire necessary permissions to digitize something or be able to document due diligence, which is an indication to others that all reasonable avenues for permission attainment were explored to their fullest extents. Copyright is a complex subject and cannot be fully fleshed out in a single book, let alone a single chapter therein. In most cases, librarians and archivists do not need to know every facet of U.S. copyright law, but they should have some understanding of its practical applications regarding educational institutions and how to avoid basic pitfalls. This chapter explores the practical application of such concepts as crafting permission request letters, managing permissions, documenting due diligence, and being responsive to claims of misuse.

Copyright Basics in the United States

U.S. copyright law is vast and poorly understood. Many librarians dedicate their entire careers to the study and application of copyright law, often in fields such as scholarly communications and open access. As more and more libraries and archives digitize their content, it is becoming more important for all librarians to have a topical working knowledge of copyright. There are three basic components of U.S. copyright law of which all librarians, especially those in digital fields, should have a general understanding:

- Fair use
- Public domain
- Section 108

Fair Use

Fair use, which is explained in section 107 of the U.S. Copyright Act of 1976, allows persons to reuse small portions of a copyrighted work so long as several factors are addressed beforehand or during a misuse claim. Fair use is vague and, like much of U.S. copyright law, can be interpreted in a variety of ways, to the benefit or detriment of the copyright holder. In general, the less that a person uses of a copyrighted work, the easier it is to claim fair use, especially if that portion has little or no effect on the market for the original (Nolo 2010a). The character of the reuse is perhaps the most crucial facet, though, and is the core of fair use. Reuse for commercial purposes is rarely, if ever, excusable under section 107. Educational institutions often claim fair use because of the nonprofit, research-oriented nature of their endeavors, citing the only benefit being to the user, who is not forced to pay for the content.

An example of fair use in a library setting would be if a librarian uploaded to You-Tube a video of an emeritus professor's memorial service in which a portion of a Duke Ellington song was played. Certain copyright owners employ algorithms that crawl services such as YouTube to identify their copyrighted works, such as a song or dialogue from a film. In this case, if the copyright holder to Duke Ellington's music claimed misuse, the library would be able to claim fair use by citing the fact that although the song is copyrighted, it was recorded incidentally (since the goal of the video was to capture a memorial service) and, as is, would not possibly damage the market appeal of the song. Furthermore, since the intention was simply to make a memorial service of a beloved professor freely available, there is no ulterior commercial motive.

Public Domain

The public domain is one of the most oft-cited facets of U.S. copyright law and, perhaps because it is one of the most well known, also one of the most incorrectly cited, too. The public domain is an "area" in which intellectual properties with no copyright or lapsed copyright reside and can be reused without permission or limit: as a general rule, all works published in the United States before 1923 or between 1923 and 1964, if copyright was not renewed (Nolo 2010b), as well as any contemporary works explicitly released directly to the public domain.

While is it actually safe to assume that a work published before 1923 is up for grabs, it is necessary to verify the copyright status of works created between 1923 and 1964. Most statuses from that period can be verified by researching the resources available from the U.S. Copyright Office at http://www.copyright.gov/records/. Most records after 1978 are viewable through the office's database, but other records, such as those from 1923 to 1964, can be found in yearly editions of *United States Copyright Catalog* or digitized versions of said catalog in the Internet Archive at http://archive.org/details/copyrightrecords.

Libraries often cite public domain when engaging in digitization activities. For example, if a library had a collection of architectural supply catalogs published in 1912, it would have no need to contact the publishers regarding digitization and public display. The same catalog published in 1925 would be subject to some amount of research, as it was published after 1922 and its copyright could have been renewed before 1964.

Section 108

Of the facets discussed thus far, section 108 is the most complex but, given its specificity to libraries, is the most important. Essentially, section 108 gives limited rights to libraries to reproduce copyrighted works for strict educational purposes. It was intended to protect libraries from being sued over making photocopies of print articles to share via interlibrary loan. Over the years, interpretation has changed to accommodate electronic formats and other rules established in the Digital Millennium Copyright Act of 1998. This is not to say that works can simply be digitized and hosted publicly so long as the organization doing so is a university or museum. In fact, to be in compliance with section 108, an institution must observe certain stipulations. For instance, libraries make copies of objects for preservation or archival purposes and, in many cases, may make copies available to library constituents but never to the general public. This stipulation is often used when migrating from obsolete formats (e.g., VHS) to modern ones (e.g., DVD or file-based digital video). In cases where migration for accessibility is the main purpose, librarians need to make a measurable effort to determine whether the work in question is available for purchase in a modern format or exists under special commercial status (e.g., no longer sold in any format; American Library Association 2013).

Section 108 would come into focus if a library were to embark on a project to convert its most used VHS tapes to DVD and/or file-based digital videos. Doing so would increase accessibility of relevant or historically important works trapped on obsolete media. To be in full compliance with section 108, a project team would have to make a concerted effort to verify that the works in question were not available on new media at a reasonable cost (comparable to the cost of the original item). If the same works on modern media could not be procured, then it would be up to the library to contact the copyright holder of each title and ask for permission to convert them to formats such as DVD or file-based digital video, which the library could host on a secure server accessible only to library patrons. Some copyright holders might give permission to convert to DVD only; some might permit creation of a hosted digital file but only if its use is limited to one patron at a time; and many others may not even be reachable. If due diligence can be proved through copious documentation, such as postmarked letters and e-mail, digitization may or may not proceed at the project team's discretion.

Due Diligence

Due diligence refers to a person's efforts to make several thorough attempts at finding the status of a potentially copyrighted work or seeking permission to reuse that work. The concept itself is not explicitly defined in U.S. copyright law but has been adopted from other laws and concepts and is in common usage. Regardless of its commonness, due diligence is just as vague as the hard-coded laws of U.S. copyright in that due diligence to one entity may be sloppy or incomplete to another. Several university libraries have made their due diligence checklists publicly available, the most robust of which is from University of Michigan at http://www.lib.umich.edu/orphan-works/documentation and is specific to that library's investigation of orphan works.

For any project that requires permission acquisition, it is wise to develop a specific set of criteria that must be fulfilled to satisfy a localized definition of due diligence. This checklist can be used as reference when seeking permission and can serve as a handy guide to the documentation that a librarian accumulates in pursuit of copyright clearance. Such a checklist might look like that in table 4.1.

If available, institutional legal counsel should be consulted when creating the form, as it might have important advice regarding wording, criteria, and appropriate time spans.

Table 4.1. Copyright Clearance: Due Diligence Checklist

CRITERIA	FULFILLED?	RESPONSE?
Copyright holder found	Yes	N/A
First letter sent	Yes	No
First e-mail sent	Yes	No
Second letter sent (30 days after first)	Yes	No
Second e-mail sent (30 days after first)	Yes	No
Permission filed	No	N/A
Due diligence	Yes	N/A

Permission Letters

Permission request letters are used to acquire digitization and electronic distribution rights for various physical and born-digital objects. In some cases, they might be individually tailored to request permission to digitize portions of a manuscript collection; in other cases, they may be form letters used to gather thousands of permissions for a retrospective thesis- and dissertation-scanning project. In all cases, however, permission request letters must be well written and detailed and express precisely the rights required. As with a copyright clearance checklist, all permission request/release forms and letters should be submitted for comment and clearance by legal counsel. Most universities and larger institutions have some form of legal counsel available to offer advice and make comments on such forms. Getting clearance from a university's attorneys, for example, is a good way to further secure the content and intent of a permission letter, especially in the event of a dispute.

The actual crafting of a permission letter does not need to be an arduous process, but it can present some challenges to individuals with little or no experience creating such forms. Luckily, there are dozens of universities and educational institutions that make digitization or electronic release forms publicly available on the Internet for perusal and inspiration. The following are examples of institutions that have created well-written and detailed permission request letters or forms:

- University of Florida Digital Library Center, http://digital.uflib.ufl.edu/procedures/copyright/
- Digital Library of Georgia, http://dlg.galileo.usg.edu/AboutDLG/DisplayPermission.html
- Hathi Trust (University of Michigan), http://www.hathitrust.org/permissions_agreement
- Xavier University, http://www.xavier.edu/library/archives/deed_of_gift_release_form.cfm%20

The example from Xavier University is actually of an electronic deed of gift—a form wielded by special collections libraries to receive collections—but includes a series of conditions, one of which is intent to digitize. Digitization permissions may not always need to be acquired after the fact, as some deeds of gift or similar contracts have a rider or condition agreement that permits digitization "at a later date."

Form letters—or permissions requests that are standard and simply cite an individual work (e.g., a thesis)—should have three basic parts:

Introduction/identification: This section includes a brief institutional statement—for example, "In an effort to increase accessibility to knowledge and better secure our unique resources, the Special Collections Department of Ivan State University Library has identified the following title as a possible entry into our digital library."

Statement of intent: This section relates to the copyright holder precisely what is being sought and the degree to which something will be digitized and made available—for example, "Ivan State University seeks nonexclusive and noncommercial internet distribution rights to ——, which will be digitized and hosted on a publicly accessible, web-based digital platform in perpetuity."

Statement of copyright holder's rights: This section, which is sometimes a separate form (e.g., signature page), outlines the copyright holder's rights—for example, "While Ivan State University exercises the right to display your work on its digital platform, you, as author, remain sole copyright holder and may at any time grant similar permission to other entities or, if necessary, cancel all contracts, at which point your work will be pulled from all publicly accessible platforms."

Naturally, each institution is unique and may require or demand different rights. Ultimately, much of the language and even some of the facets could be up to an institution's legal counsel. It is important to remember that permission request forms are simply a means to an end, which is a marked increase in accessibility of a theretofore inaccessible resource. It should be communicated in all permission requests that the goal of a project is not to take credit for the creation a resource but to offer the privileged service to preserve and present that resource on behalf of the copyright holder. The goal, after all, is not notoriety but managed knowledge distribution.

🌀 Key Points

Planning for digitization seems like a daunting task, especially if resources are sparse and experiences are narrow. Digitization, however, is a wide field with hundreds of practitioners, many of which are just as inexperienced. Luckily, there are many libraries and institutions that are highly experienced and usually willing to share lessons and advice. The Internet is rife with examples of course integration, collaborations, and even specific project documentation, much of which is publicly accessible on the principle that free authoritative information will assist others in building collections and furthering that information.

The key points to this chapter are as follows:

- Assess a project's feasibility by understanding its boundaries regarding technology, personnel, and overall cost. If technology is owned or attainable and personnel can be shifted or hired with reasonable strain on financial and time resources, a project is likely feasible.

- Plan for value-added features. Incorporating features such as course integration and prescribed collaboration into a project can not only offset costs but also lend esteem to an endeavor and widen its reach.
- Always consider copyright and permission acquisition to be the essential pieces to forming a responsible digital project. Securing legitimate rights to publish and preserve objects, be they audiovisual or otherwise, is sometimes overlooked but should always be a component of any project, even if rights are assumed, as conditions change and it never hurts to be absolutely certain when it comes to copyright.
- Careful consideration of these points is crucial in establishing a cogent plan for a project that will succeed or fail based, not on planning, but on the content and goals themselves.

References

American Library Association. 2013. "Section 108 Photocopying by Libraries and Archives." http://www.ala.org/advocacy/copyright/dmca/section108.

Harpold, T. 2007. "LIT3400: Interdisciplinary Topics in Literature—Technologies of the Book." University of Florida. http://www.clas.ufl.edu/users/tharpold/courses/fall07/lit3400/index.html.

Nolo. 2010a. "Educational Uses of Non-coursepack Materials." Stanford University Libraries. http://fairuse.stanford.edu/Copyright_and_Fair_Use_Overview/chapter7/7-b.html#1.

———. 2010b. "Welcome to the Public Domain." Stanford University Libraries. http://fairuse.stanford.edu/Copyright_and_Fair_Use_Overview/chapter8/8-a.html.

CHAPTER 5

Digitization: Managing Digitization, Selecting Equipment, and Applying Standards

THE REAL-WORLD PROCESSES in managing the digitization of audiovisual objects are unlike most other digital capture routines. While digital imaging relies on the latest hardware to faithfully reproduce digital copies of antique books and maps, much of the equipment used in the capture of audiovisual resources is decidedly antique itself and far more difficult to acquire. The reason for dependence on effectively antique hardware is inherent in the media of audiovisual objects. While it is fairly easy to photograph an antique book with a variety of imaging devices, cutting-edge or otherwise, an individual attempting to capture content from an obsolete U-Matic videotape has only one option: find a U-Matic deck, which is itself obsolete. Typically, the only components of an audiovisual digitization unit considered cutting-edge are the software used to transcode digital files from one format/codec to another and the capture devices, which are the translators between playback devices and computers. This setup, while seemingly convoluted, is really quite simple and can easily be scaled and modified to support a variety of institutions. Much of what a person needs to know about audiovisual digitization need never extend beyond that which can be found in a basic overview. This chapter gives such an overview so that librarians reading it will feel comfortable enough to begin asking more complex questions of colleagues, professional and amateur, and feel confident that what they have learned will allow them to speak intelligently about audiovisual digitization.

This chapter addresses the practicalities in digitizing analog audiovisual resources and manipulating born-digital audiovisual resources. The first section, In-House versus Vended Digitization, delves into the differences between digitizing audiovisual resources in-house and turning to a qualified vendor. Both approaches have strengths and weaknesses, and an institution can often succeed by implementing either or both. The next section, Working with Vendors, goes deeper into the vendor-institution relationship and provides insight into making that relationship long lasting and productive. The subsequent section, Selecting Equipment for In-House Digitization, makes suggestions and recommendations on selecting hardware for managing digitization in-house and where to acquire it. Then, Selecting and Applying Standards for Digitization details and distills audiovisual capture criteria. Finally, sample workflows are presented to help visualize how equipment, standards, and processes converge into a practical series of operations.

In-House versus Vended Digitization

The decision to digitize analog audiovisual resources in-house or turn to a competent vendor is not one to make lightly. A variety of factors can influence an institution to proceed down one path, the other, or both, but equal consideration should be given to each alternative. It is important to consider the startup costs associated with in-house digitization, as well as the lack of control when using a vendor. Concessions do not always have to be made, but a librarian must weigh all options carefully and determine what is most beneficial and, perhaps more important, what behooves the material. This section compares and contrasts the fundamental differences between in-house and vended digitization and sets the foundation for the third and fourth sections, which focus on the specifics of either path.

In-House Digitization

In-house digitization, while certainly more of an undertaking in some respects than vended digitization, can empower an institution to have total control over its collection and the digital results thereof. A librarian can select as much or as little equipment as is required to complete a project or support a program without having to pay for the intangible costs associated with a vendor's overhead. Managing one's digitization in-house provides total control over both the product of capture (the digital file) and its security (responsibility for custody). These two benefits are often reason enough to at least have limited infrastructure for supporting in-house digitization, as the higher initial cost of in-house digitization might be preferable to any loss in control when using a vendor. Furthermore, a library that wields its own audiovisual digitization program can, after successful applications of its tools and trials, reach out to other departments, programs, or institutions and assist them in their initiatives. This can build goodwill among organizations and support a network of cooperatives with similar interests and goals.

Table 5.1. Common Equipment and Software Considerations for Audiovisual Digitization

CONSIDERATION	TYPICAL COST	USE	EXAMPLE	SAMPLE COST
Playback device	$300–$35,000	Plays back analog media format	Sony BVW-75 Betacam Deck	$1,500 (used)
Capture card, dongle, or device	$35–$150	Converts analog signal to digital; interfaces with computer	Happauge Colossus	$150 (new)
Transcoder	Typically free and open source	Software to transcode raw capture data to usable archival and delivery files	FFmpeg	Free
Video-editing software	$100–$1,000	Used to create delivery files or edit video	Final Cut Pro	$300

While there are certainly many benefits to having total control over a collection and its digitization, such control comes at a high initial cost and, depending on how such a program progresses, relatively high recurring costs as well. These costs, initial and continual, are not just monetary but can also be calculated in thought and time: both valuable commodities not always in surplus. The monetary costs are, however, the easiest to calculate, and they include equipment, software, training, and labor. Table 5.1 illustrates common equipment and software considerations.

Table 5.1 takes into account only a single piece of equipment, but it is likely that an institution beginning a program of this sort will need to purchase several different playback devices (video cassette recorders, audiocassette decks, reel-to-reel players, etc.). Labor and training costs are slightly more difficult to calculate or exemplify, as they can fluctuate depending on whether an institution has available expertise on hand, must employ training courses, or has to hire an expert. Hiring an individual to manage audiovisual digitization can cost tens of thousands of dollars per year and so indicates a serious commitment to building and maintaining an in-house digitization program. Such a venture is likely to be preferred by institutions with very large audiovisual collections and a vested interest in growing them. These costs and ways to mitigate them are covered more deeply later in this chapter.

Vended Digitization

For institutions with small audiovisual collections or even those simply wishing to digitize a high number of videotapes or audiocassettes very quickly, a vendor is likely to be a better choice than investing in equipment and software that may not be used again. Audiovisual digitization vendors typically own an array of legacy playback equipment and can digitize most common—and many uncommon—audiovisual formats. While most vendors in this field are competent, reliable, and highly professional, there is always a risk that assets could be poorly captured, damaged, or even destroyed. Limiting the kinds of materials sent to a vendor can mitigate these risks. For example, a library may decide that it wants to digitize for the purposes of providing streaming video for its entire collection of documentaries, all of which are on VHS tapes. It is highly unlikely that these hypothetical VHS tapes, while functionally obsolete, are necessarily rare. In this case, it would be easy to send these tapes to a trusted vendor and set aside worries of losing fragile, rare, or irreplaceable objects. However, more thought should be devoted to sending a vendor one-of-a-kind audio recordings on quarter-inch audiotape, for example, the damage or destruction of which might be a significant blow to a library's collection or reputation. It is wise to research a vendor, form a relationship with its managers, and build trust.

Vendor pricing varies from company to company but typically includes costs per object or length of content. For example, digitizing a thirty-minute Betacam SP tape will cost more than digitizing one half as long. Formats that are more difficult to handle, such as 16-mm film, will likely cost considerably more to digitize than formats such as VHS, which are sturdier and functionally easier to capture. Vendors also typically charge to make reproductions or conversions of one physical medium to another (e.g., VHS to DVD). Another consideration is that shipping large quantities of material can become very expensive in and of itself and is rarely a service covered by vendors. The peculiarities of working with vendors are covered more deeply later in the chapter.

Utilizing In-House Program and Vendors

Many institutions, rather than being wholly dependent on either their own equipment or the services of a vendor, opt to pursue a two-pronged approach: digitize some things in-house and send others to a trusted vendor. This approach is particularly helpful to institutions that have mixed audiovisual collections consisting of rare objects and common but simply obsolete resources and are more concerned with striking a balance between control over its assets and being cost-effective. No matter the preference of an institution, it is wise to keep options open: a library with an advanced audiovisual digitization lab may suffer equipment malfunctions during a tight production schedule and would benefit from a strong relationship with a vendor who can fulfill the requirements of that library's project or program.

Simply having the option to utilize a vendor rather than in-house resources is a wise practical consideration. It simply is not efficient to purchase a costly film-to-digital video transfer system to digitize a few cans of archival 16-mm film. Most audiovisual vendors are more than capable of digitizing a variety of film gauges and quantities and have already made investments in equipment. Furthermore, building a productive relationship with a vendor or vendors is a sign that the institution is serious about the well-being and permanence of its audiovisual resources, as well as its relevance among its peers.

Working with Vendors

Audiovisual vendors run the gamut from two-person shops capable of transferring VHS and other consumer audiovisual formats to DVDs and digital file-based formats to large laboratories focusing on film and digitizing less well-known formats, such as type C magnetic tape. There is no complete clearinghouse of audiovisual conversion vendors, but many universities maintain publicly available lists that can serve as a jumping-off point for an institution not familiar with the industry. The actual act of selecting a vendor should not be made lightly or at random; an institution should contact several vendors and ask for quotes in determining pricing and then compare the results to the reputation of each one, not necessarily just selecting the vendor with the lowest prices. This section delves into how to find vendors, what requests and considerations to make when working with one, and, finally, how to maintain a productive relationship with a vendor or vendors.

Finding a Vendor

Choosing a vendor to digitize any number of archival audiovisual objects can be an intimidating and confusing task. It is not uncommon to have questions:

- Will the vendor take good care of the materials and not damage them?
- Will the vendor deliver in a timely manner?
- Will I lose control over the final product?
- How do I know this vendor is the right vendor?

It is impossible to answer such questions with precision, but simply researching several such entities and asking them as many reasonable questions as possible can mitigate the risks inherent in entrusting another entity with one's materials. Vendors in the realm of audiovisual digitization are generally very professional and, given the rare skills involved in such work, often work together to ensure that the industry is one of high repute.

Perhaps the best way to begin the selection process is to inquire with peer institutions and colleagues about their experiences in working with audiovisual vendors. Academic institutions rarely officially endorse one vendor over another, but they are often willing to divulge their experiences—positive or negative—and can serve as a solid basis for one's exploration of the vendor environment. For educational purposes, some larger institutions that are involved in a high number of conversion projects have published noncomprehensive lists of audiovisual vendors, which can serve as good starting points for researching the field.

The University of Michigan's Library Digital Conversion Unit maintains a list entitled "Vendors for Audio Digitization and Preservation" (University of Michigan n.d.). That document is part of an academic institution's library documentation and serves as a point of reference for anyone interested. Another place to find the names of audiovisual vendors is in federal or consortial technical documentation. For example, the Consortium of Academic and Research Libraries in Illinois published a document entitled "Guidelines for the Creation of Digital Collections: Digitization Best Practices for Moving Images," which includes an appendix listing select vendors (CARLI Digital Collections Users' Group 2010).

These documents and others are good places to start looking for audiovisual vendors, and it is wise to contact and consult more than one. Pricing among vendors can be very competitive, but the right vendor often exists at the confluence of low cost, high quality, and responsiveness. While this point of merging is not always attainable, it is best to favor the latter two caveats, as a high-quality result will always be worth a reasonable fee and responsiveness and communication from a vendor cannot be priced.

Communicating with a Vendor

While some vendors may be willing to make a trip to personally assess your audiovisual collection and provide you with a quote based on their expert firsthand opinion, it will more likely be incumbent on you to accurately describe the types of materials earmarked for conversion and their conditions via telephone or e-mail. Many vendors understand that the average individual may not be able to differentiate between film gauges or broadcast tape formats, but any information about the media can assist the vendor in making an accurate quote. Using what you have learned from chapter 2 and the myriad format identification resources that it references, you should be able to provide an accurate description of the resources you wish to digitize.

In general, vendors will want to know the following details:

- Types of media formats included in the project (e.g., videotape variety, film)
- Number of total objects, as well as number of each format
- General condition of each format type's constituents
- Any time constraints
- Product expectations/requests (e.g., DVD copies, final format needs)

It is best to present this information in the form of a multispreadsheet workbook, with one sheet dedicated to each format type and each entry clearly represented by a name, number, or other identifier that ties it to the physical item. Table 5.2 illustrates how such a sheet might look. It shows the running time of each object—an estimate of which is often requested by vendors, as some charge conversions by a tape's length—as well as a column for a file name, which is an indication to the vendor that you want the resultant files to follow a particular naming scheme. Such a document should also serve as a packing list and manifest.

While many vendors follow a basic routine that results in standard digital file formats, it is wise to indicate the formats you desire and if they differ greatly from the vendor's standard so that an agreement can be reached. Generally, vendors supply their clients with an uncompressed, or lossless, digital file used for archiving and one smaller, lossy derivative file used for access and distribution. The specific codecs and formats of preference differ from vendor to vendor but can surely be specified by the client based on his or her own preference. It is in this discussion that you should also indicate whether your project necessitates the creation of DVDs or other optical media to which the original analog formats should be converted. Finally, arrangements should be made for storage of the digital files on external hard drives, on ones that you either provide or purchase through the vendor, if such a service is available. Keep in mind that the resultant digital files could be very large and, depending on the number of total files, might require several terabytes of hard drive space. Eventually, your vendor will provide you a contract or something similar, which you should carefully review for all requested job specifications.

Table 5.2. Sample Item Inventory for Vendor

OBJECT NAME	FORMAT	CONDITION	RUNNING TIME	FILE NAME	NOTES
Battleship Potemkin	VHS	Frame dropout during play, tape appears damaged	75 minutes	00001	No case
Interview 005	Betacam SP	Cannot play, object appears to be in good condition	30 minutes	00002	
Scrimshaw for Beginners	U-Matic	Video plays, some tracking issues, object in good condition	60 minutes	00003	
"TEST"	Betacam SP	Cannot play, object appears to be in good condition	15 minutes	00004	

⑥ Selecting Equipment for In-House Digitization

Whether you are pursuing a comprehensive in-house digitization program or simply need a few pieces of essential equipment for the odd videotape or audiocassette, this section covers the basics of selection and specification for either path. In many cases, the equipment detailed or even suggested in this section will not be easily attainable through conventional means, such as resellers or manufacturers, but suggestions are made on places to inquire when looking for hard-to-find equipment that is no longer manufactured. Common specifications are laid out relative to various use cases that will change depending on your needs. This is by no means an exhaustive list but provides general advice on the most common equipment arrangements, specifications, and problems therein.

While there are hundreds of pieces of equipment that one could ultimately accumulate for audiovisual capture and an even greater number of configurations, there are two main categories under which all capture technology falls:

Playback device: any piece of equipment capable of replaying an audiovisual medium.

Capture device: any piece of equipment capable of interfacing between a playback device and a computer system to facilitate recording and/or encoding of an audiovisual medium.

The nomenclature for these categories may change from vendor to vendor and locale to locale, but if one considers the definitions as immutable, acquisition of the equipment therein should require little or no translation.

Playback Devices

Playback devices are exactly that: devices that allow playback of media. This broad category can include anything from handheld microcassette recorders to expensive film capture systems. Many devices are capable of recording on their native formats as well as playing them back, which is true of VCRs, audiocassette recorders, and myriad others. This is important to note because, much like scanning equipment used to capture books and photographs, audiovisual playback devices are just as capable of damaging or destroying a media object. In the case of audiovisual media—unlike books or other paper objects—the types of devices used to play them back and, ultimately, assist in their capture and preservation were likely used in their creation. Great care should be taken to ensure that each playback device is deployed in such a way that accidental record-overs are unlikely and, most important, that technicians and operators are thoroughly trained in proper handling of media objects and playback devices.

Fairly common devices, such as VHS VCRs, can still be acquired with a minimum of labor and expense, but other devices, such as reel-to-reel players, are no longer manufactured en masse and can be difficult to find and costly to acquire. This is perhaps the most important factor in whether to maintain a functioning in-house digitization program: while some of the more common playback devices are still relatively inexpensive and easy to find, almost any legacy audiovisual playback device that you can acquire will be in the secondhand market. The warranties on most, if not all, will be void because of repair or age, and the costs for rehabilitating certain playback devices (e.g., Betacam SP decks) can vary wildly but are often more expensive than the purchase of a new secondhand device.

Unlike many other digitization systems and subrealms that are fairly recent technological and systemic enterprises, audiovisual capture systems must necessarily consist of newer capture equipment and much older playback devices, a configuration that increases the complexity of preservation and increases the likelihood of component failure. If such resources are available, it is wise to consult with audiovisual engineers or technicians affiliated with your library who can provide free advice on the specific malfunctions common to certain devices and their experiences in working with them.

The following sections detail some of the most common devices that a library will need to possess should it begin a small- to medium-capacity audiovisual capture program, the average prices for each, and general considerations.

VHS VCRs and Tapes

VHS-playing VCRs were easily the most common and successful video playback devices from the early 1980s until the rise of DVDs and DVD players in the final years of the twentieth century. They were a fixture in many North American homes and were used in a variety of capacities, including playing back rented or purchased VHS tapes, reviewing VHS recordings made with a handheld video camera, and recording directly from a television signal. While many persons are familiar with the consumer-grade VHS VCR (figure 5.1, left), fewer are familiar with professional decks (figure 5.1, right). The former were marketed to and purchased by the majority of consumers during the medium's heyday and vary greatly in quality, functionality, and lifespan. The latter were marketed to and purchased by enthusiasts and audiovisual professionals. A third level of quality and engineering is often referred to as "prosumer grade," which includes VHS VCRs with all-common consumer-grade features and a handful of professional ones: the most common of which being time-based correctors, mechanisms that compensate for mechanical instabilities inherent in VCRs and improve the quality of playback (see http://mediacollege.com), and digital noise reducers, which filter out different kinds of noise from a medium's audio signal (see http://digitalfaq.com).

While a high-quality consumer-grade deck is handy when no greater tools exist, it is preferable to spend a little time, energy, and money acquiring at least a prosumer-grade VHS VCR. Given the purpose of audiovisual capture in most libraries—preservation—it is desirable to attain the highest quality possible when playing back and capturing a VHS tape, thus increasing the quality of the final archival digital file. Generally speaking, the better quality of deck, the better looking and more robust the final digital file. In any scenario, it is also desirable to acquire a VCR capable of playing back S-VHS (Super VHS) tapes. While not hugely successful as a consumer format, S-VHS tapes saw much adoption among enthusiasts and professionals. Such a VCR is also capable of playing back standard VHS cassette tapes. Either format is likely to be found among the resources in the archives, special collections, or general circulating collections of most libraries.

Figure 5.1. Consumer and Professional VHS VCRs.

The following list summarizes the most important features to consider when purchasing a professional, prosumer, or consumer VHS VCR:

- Time-based correction (devices can be purchased separately and run between playback device and capture device)
- S-VHS playback
- S-Video-out connections (video)
- RCA-out connections (audio/video)
- Digital noise reduction
- Hi-fi (high-fidelity) audio playback
- Four playback heads

The majority of the aforementioned features are standard on professional and prosumer decks made in the 1990s, but it is always wise to thoroughly investigate the specifications on any deck, regardless of apparent age.

Prices for VHS VCRs vary wildly among consumer, prosumer, and professional models. Consumer S-VHS VCRs can still be purchased as new items from major retailers, though they are most often a component of a VCR-DVD combination deck. According to BroadcastStore.com (http://www.broadcaststore.com), prices for such decks run between $80 to $200 depending on the manufacturer and features. Professional decks are no longer produced and are available only in the secondhand market. According to a popular online reseller of audiovisual equipment, professional decks can vary in price between $600 and more than $2,000.

Betacam VCRs and Tapes

Betacam is a high-quality half-inch tape format common in the broadcasting industry and still used today by video professionals and archivists. It comes in many variations:

- *Betacam:* analog, medium quality
- *Betacam SP:* analog, high quality
- *Betacam SX:* digital, higher quality, transitional
- *Digital Betacam:* digital, highest quality

All these formats were or are currently in use in the broadcasting industry and exhibit much higher quality and recording fidelity than any VHS or three-quarter-inch videotape formats (Texas Commission on the Arts 2004, 18). Because of the format family's inherent high quality, long lifespan, and fidelity, a librarian or archivist is very likely to encounter such tapes in journalism libraries, music archives, and special collections.

Betacam (figure 5.2, left) should not be confused with Betamax (figure 5.2, right), a consumer-grade tape format common before the rise of VHS in the early 1980s. While mechanically identical, tapes recorded on a Betamax device cannot be replayed on a Betacam deck and vice versa, although the tapes themselves can be interchanged when blank. It is important to note that only the latest Digital Betacam players can play all earlier Betacam formats. For example, a Digital Betacam tape cannot be replayed in a Betacam SP player, but a Betacam tape can be played back on a Digital Betacam deck (Texas Commission on the Arts 2004, 27). Because of this cascading backward compatibility, purchasing a Digital Betacam deck will increase the likelihood that tapes discovered in an archive can be replayed and captured.

Figure 5.2. Betacam and Betamax VCRs.

The following list summarizes the most important features to consider when purchasing a Betacam deck (assuming purchase of Digital Betacam device):

- Backward compatibility with Betacam family
- High-definition upconvert
- SDI and analog composite inputs

Given the flexibility of Digital Betacam decks, it is not advisable to seek out older Betacam devices, as they will severely limit your ability to capture a variety of formats within the Betacam family. This is dependent on one's collection, however, and a simple Betacam or Betacam SP deck may be sufficient. In general, when a Betacam or Betacam SP deck is being purchased, there are few feature considerations to be made. While there are thousands of models of VHS VCRs with only feature enhancements to distinguish them, Betacam family decks exist only as professional tools and even the lowest-end model of any particular brand has the basic features that an archivist or librarian needs to perform simple capture tasks.

Betacam players are easily the most expensive VCRs, and according to Broadcast-Store.com, low-end models in the secondhand market can range from $500 to $2,000 and high-end models can exceed $5,000. Although the most versatile and advanced in the Betacam family, Digital Betacam decks can cost upward of $15,000 for the most feature-rich systems and only slightly less for basic models.

U-Matic VCRs and Tapes

Common in the 1970s, U-Matic VCRs were widely used in the broadcast and video production industries. Unlike its successor technology, Betacam, U-Matic played and recorded on a slightly wider, three-quarter-inch cassette tape format. As one of the first technologies utilizing encased videotape as a recoding medium and not requiring development like film formats, U-Matic (figure 5.3) was very popular among television producers and videographers with fewer financial resources. The format also saw a lot of use in the education sector and is likely to be encountered by archivists and librarians at postsecondary educational institutions (Texas Commission on the Arts 2004, 11). Given its use by some as a transitional medium when mastering or archiving audio recordings from other media, it is not uncommon to find U-Matic videotapes with no video signal and carrying only a full-length audio recording. Despite its low cost and myriad uses, U-Matic fell out of favor in the 1980s as it lost ground to higher-quality formats such as Betacam.

The following list summarizes the most important features to consider when purchasing a U-Matic deck:

Figure 5.3. U-Matic VCR.

- Front-loading (top-loading units require an adapter to play U-Matic S tapes)
- Time-based correction

Like Betacam family players, U-Matic decks were produced for only the professional market, and even the lowest-end models are sufficient for simple capture tasks. Specifying and purchasing U-Matic players generally poses fewer roadblocks than do Betacam devices. U-Matic decks were manufactured with fewer variations and did not experience the same level of format modification as Betacam. While later-model U-Matic players had more features improving tape stability and tracking than did older ones, the tapes themselves did not change. For the purposes of portability, a smaller three-quarter-inch tape called U-Matic S was developed, but even this smaller tape could be played back in either the top- or front-loading U-Matic decks. U-Matic players are becoming harder to find as time progresses and can post as much of a financial barrier as purchasing a Betacam family deck. According to BroadcastStore.com, prices for U-Matic decks range from $700 to well over $3,000.

Reel-to-Reel Audiotape Recorders

Reel-to-reel audiotape recorders and players are a class of device used for recording and playing back a variety of tape formats stored on reels. For the purposes of this book, the most common of these formats is quarter-inch audiotape. This format was widely used from the 1950s until the mid-1970s when cassette formats supplanted reel-based media. While not technically a professional format, quarter-inch tape was used widely by amateurs, educational institutions, and historians because of its low cost, high capacity, and life span. While certainly unwieldy to use, reel-to-reel players can be very helpful to an institution with a focus on oral histories or other audio-only collections (see textbox 5.1), as it is likely that the majority of the items therein will exist as quarter-inch-tape reels.

Unlike the VCRs detailed in the previous sections, reel-to-reel players (figure 5.4) are less intimidating to specify, as they were produced mostly for amateur operations and have only the most basic functions: recording, simple editing, and playback. The most important consideration to make when purchasing a reel-to-reel player is that it does indeed play the format most common in your collections. There were a variety of audiotape formats, and most reel-to-reel players can only accommodate one. There is little or no variation in players that would affect simple capture tasks.

TEXTBOX 5.1.

PROJECT STARTERS: COMMUNITY HISTORIES

Description

A library or archive, regardless of its institutional affiliation, should strive to have some connection to the local community of which it is certainly a part. An effort to document the visual public history of a city or community can be an overwhelming project but can be tailored to address specific groups or neighborhoods first. A project such as this could simply involve the digitization of owned collections relevant to a specific area of a community or could expand to involve other institutions. Perhaps the best and most exciting part of documenting community histories is the involvement of members of the communities in question. One way to engage members of a community is to solicit the submission of audiovisual (and other) resources to your library for inclusion in a curated project. Such a project has high potential for longevity, as individuals will most likely remain interested in the collection given their vested interest in its makeup and use. The project materials themselves could be curated in dozens of different ways, but since communities are typically tied to a specific geographic area with differing contexts and interpretations, a map-based presentation mechanism would be ideal.

Common Sources

- University archives
- Community organizations
- Private individuals

Common Physical and Digital Formats

- Audiocassettes
- VHS videocassettes
- VHS-C videocassettes
- Born-digital video and audio files
- MiniDV videocassettes
- Hi-8 videocassettes

Project Hurdles

- Deciding on permissions and ownership of donated/loaned materials
- Managing influxes of data
- Effective and sensitive curation

Community History Projects:

- Creating Your Community/Creating Communities, Denver Public Library, http://creating communities.denverlibrary.org
- Oberlin College LGBT Community History Project, Oberlin College, http://www.oberlin lgbt.org/content/
- Historypin, We Are What We Do, http://www.historypin.com

Figure 5.4. Reel-to-Reel Player.

While less intimidating than Betacam or U-Matic decks, reel-to-reel players can still pose a significant financial hurdle. According to a popular Internet auction site, many brands can be found for around $450, but they are not always fully functional and may require repairs. The more historically robust brands and models therein can still cost upward of $1,000 in the secondhand market and, because of their construction, are less prone to mechanical failure (http://www.broadcaststore.com).

Audiocassette Recorders and Tapes

Sometimes called a compact cassette, the common audiocassette is one of the most successful and widespread media ever to be manufactured. Used by professionals and amateurs alike, audiocassettes are capable of storing stereophonic or monophonic information at a range of speeds and lengths. Generally, the audiocassettes that one encounters in a library setting are from the 1980s and 1990s, can accommodate between 30 and 45 minutes per side, and are represented by hundreds of brands. While some such tapes in your collection may have been recorded professionally or used to remaster quarter-inch audiotape, many were likely recorded using simple handheld cassette recorders without an external microphone.

Due to their popularity and segmentation into consumer and professional models, audiocassette players (figure 5.5) are as voluminous in availability as VHS VCRs. They exist at a variety of levels and are represented by dozens of brands, but most are easily identifiable as audiocassette recorders. While a small-scale digitization effort can certainly make do with an inexpensive handheld recorder/player, it is desirable to invest just

Figure 5.5. Professional Audiocassette Recorder/Player.

slightly more money in a high-end player. Some features to consider when purchasing an audiocassette deck are as follows:

- Two tape slots
- Auto-reverse (plays opposite side of tape without need for flipping)
- RCA (red and white) stereo outputs
- Noise reduction (often found in Dolby-equipped decks)

With the aforementioned features—which are found in hundreds of players—you will be able to capture most audiocassette tapes with a high degree of fidelity and minimal postprocessing. The majority of audiocassette decks in this array will range in price from $100 to $500 in the secondhand market and at specialty resellers. Some similar consumer-grade systems are still manufactured, though often in combination with CD players and highly touted "cassette-to-MP3" converters falling in the same price range as professional decks.

Marketplaces

The secondhand market for the aforementioned devices can be intimidating and, in some cases, hard to define. Online auction houses such as eBay are good places to start, but as with any such venue, there is a high degree of risk involved: aside from the obvious risk of not getting what one paid for, prices may be grossly inflated from the item's actual value. It is wise to consider a variety of alternatives to purchasing such equipment from auction sites. There are a number of reputable dealers in used audiovisual playback devices that have web and brick-and-mortar presences and can offer professional advice to customers.

Besides the obvious marketplaces, there are venues that are likely to be overlooked but always worthy of consideration. Many academic institutions maintain surplus property departments that manage the accumulation, redistribution, and sometimes resale of surplus equipment. Legacy audiovisual components often find their ways to these departments and go unnoticed for many years before being discarded. Institutions with robust journalism and mass communication programs are likely to have had bevies of such equipment and, as they updated standards over the decades, relinquished much of it to surplus property managers. It is wise to inquire within one's institution before venturing out into the retail world.

Finally, things as mundane as garage sales, swap meets, and flea markets are often good places to find older audiovisual equipment. Such places are more likely to have common consumer-level audiocassette players and VHS VCRs than the higher-level devices described earlier, but simply investigating these venues can sometimes yield unexpected results. At the very least, audiovisual equipment found and purchased from flea markets and garage sales can be used for spare parts and as backups for higher-quality devices.

Cables and Connectors

Each of the previously discussed playback devices utilizes a variety of input and output cables. These cables can be used to record on the device (input) or play back media (output). In any case, all cables essentially serve the same purpose: to move data from one device to another, the only considerations being what kinds of data and in what direction. Some cables can transport only audio or video signals, while some can accommodate both. Technically speaking, connector types and signal standards are different, and two or more of the latter can be transmitted through one of the former. However, this guide will cover only the most common connector-standard combinations. The most important note, though, is what specific outputs your playback device has and what inputs your capture device allows. The following are the most common output types found on a variety of devices:

RCA: can carry either composite video (yellow cable) or component video (green, red, and blue cables), as well as stereo audio (red and white cables). This connector type is perhaps the most common among consumer-grade devices (figure 5.6, left).

TRS: sometimes called a stereo connector, TRS connectors typically carry audio signals and are most often seen on instrument cables, headphones, and a variety of devices for the purpose of accepting an incoming audio signal. The connector comes in either a quarter-inch or 3.5-mm format (figure 5.6, right).

BNC: a variation on coaxial radio frequency cables like ones used to connect antennae to televisions, BNC connectors are found on serial digital interface and simple analog video cables to carry video signals, as well as red and white stereo cables (like those utilized in the RCA type) to carry audio signals. BNC connectors are typically

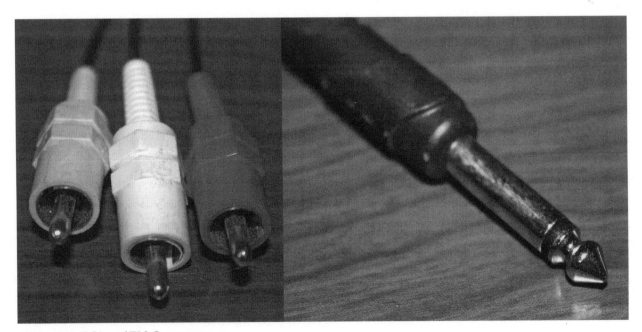

Figure 5.6. RCA and TRS Connectors.

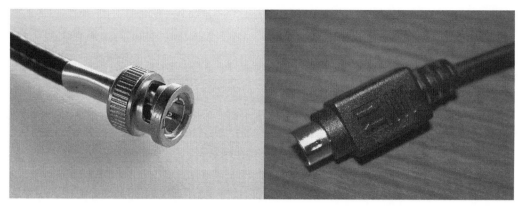

Figure 5.7. BNC and S-Video Connectors.

equipped with a quick-release lock mechanism that allows them to be securely connected to a device without being as difficult to remove as coaxial cables (figure 5.7).

S-Video: these four-pin connectors are used exclusively for the transmission of video signals. S-Video is capable of carrying a slightly higher-quality signal than composite RCA connectors but a lower-quality one than component RCA (figure 5.7).

HDMI: of the connectors/standards on this list, HDMI (high-definition multimedia interface) is the most versatile and advanced. It can transmit high-definition video, audio, and other data through a single connector. It will not be found on legacy audiovisual equipment but is likely to be a component of capture devices (figure 5.8).

XLR: used to carry balanced audio signals, XLR connectors and cables are most commonly found on devices capable of recording audio signals from external input devices such as microphones. The connectors themselves can come in a variety of pin configurations, but most of the devices described in earlier sections will accommodate the three-pin variety, sometimes combined with a TRS input (figure 5.8).

One thing to remember when assembling a playback-capture setup is that there are adapters for most connectors and standards. Even though a certain connection seems unbridgeable, there almost always exists an adapter capable of making a square peg fit into a round hole or, as the case may be, an XLR output to a RCA input. If the connection required cannot be solved by one of the thousands of premade adaptations, many companies will custom-make ad hoc adapters. The situations most likely to pose connection conflicts occur when bridging an audiovisual playback deck to a modern capture device. The following section briefly describes the two basic categories of capture device most often employed in small- to medium-sized operations.

Figure 5.8. HDMI and XLR Connectors.

Capture Devices

For a computer to receive and process audiovisual data from a playback device, a capture device must be utilized. Most modern computers are equipped with simple 3.5-mm TRS audio inputs (microphone jacks) that allow one to capture audio streams from CD players, phonographs, or anything with a compatible output. Video streams from devices generally require a wider variety of inputs that most computers are not initially equipped to accept. To accept these signals, either an external capture device or an internal capture card must be installed, forming the bridge from the playback deck to the computer to the computer's audiovisual capture software. In essence, a capture device, despite its configuration, creates compatible connections where none existed before, either via common computer inputs such as USB or by interfacing directly with a computer's motherboard, as in a PCI capture card. Some capture devices also include an encoder, or set of software that converts raw audiovisual signals into compressed ones for use in a variety of application. Depending on your individual applications, some devices may be more desirable than others.

Internal Capture Cards

Internal capture cards look much like standard video graphics cards but function in different ways. While video graphics cards accept a standard VGA (video graphics array) or DVI (digital video interchange) signal from a monitor, capture cards convert several kinds of signals across a variety of connectors into a VGA, DVI, or HDMI connection. Most such cards accomplish this by being equipped with a dongle, or a breakout cable, which is a small device capable of turning one input/output into an array (figure 5.9).

Most capture cards are equipped with at least S-Video and the component and composite varieties of RCA connectors. Among these connectors, it should be possible to accommodate most audiovisual playback decks, though some ad hoc adaptors may be necessary. Some capture cards are hardwired to act as encoders and cannot capture raw video without encoding and compressing it. The same is also true of some external capture devices, but options within either category are wide. Depending on the brand and

Figure 5.9. Common Internal Capture Card.

Figure 5.10. Common External Capture Device.

configuration, capture cards tend to be slightly more costly than external ones but have advantages in build quality, brand consistency, and software.

External Capture Devices

Unlike internal capture cards, external capture devices are stand-alone tools that create a bridge between a playback deck and a computer system. Such devices often connect to a computer via USB, Firewire, or other common inputs and are powered independently. Some are hardwired to encode raw video into formats such as MP4 and cannot be used to capture raw video directly. Units can range from small, thumb-sized devices with breakout cables to much larger, modem-sized units with a variety of direct inputs. This assortment in size, shape, and capability creates a much wider field of options for a librarian looking to capture video (figure 5.10). However, given the wider assortment, there are a number of brands and builds with significant shortcomings. Thus, it is wise to closely investigate each unit under consideration and contact others who have engaged in similar pursuits.

External capture devices tend to be less expensive than their internal counterparts and are currently more popular. This popularity is likely due to the overall ease of use inherent in the installation and configuration of external devices. Internal capture cards may be intimidating pieces of equipment for beginners, and given their need to connect directly to a computer's motherboard, their improper installation is likelier. One must make a variety of compromises when purchasing a device of any category, but each person or institution must make determinations based on need, skill level, and compatibility. Table 5.3 highlights some of the pros and cons of each capture device type vis-à-vis one another.

Clearly, cases can be made for either item category. It should be noted that although many external capture devices are somewhat limited by the connection speeds between themselves and their attached computers, many new connection protocols, such as Thunderbolt and USB 3.0, have arisen and may help to mitigate said limitations or circumvent them entirely. If an operation has the financial wherewithal to do so, it is wise to purchase both an internal and an external capture device with nearly identical specifications and compare their real-world capabilities on the same machine.

The final component to a working audiovisual capture system is a software program capable of communicating with the capture device and facilitating the recording of any incoming signals. Many of the best options for this kind of software are free of cost but

Table 5.3. Internal versus External Capture Devices

PROS: INTERNAL	CONS: INTERNAL
Faster	Can be difficult to install
Good brand reputations	Shrinking market share
Better software drivers	More expensive
PROS: EXTERNAL	**CONS: EXTERNAL**
Mobility	Proliferation of poor-quality devices
Easy to install	Require faster processing speed
Less expensive	Performance constrained by connection to computer

may require some time and effort in deciphering. Some are capable of encoding only incoming signals in a certain set of codecs and formats; others are designed to accept raw signals and do very little in the way of compression. The myriad approaches to this facet are covered briefly in the next section.

Software

Audiovisual capture software is a very broad field and can include everything from expensive video-editing suites such as Final Cut Pro to free transcoding software such as FFmpeg. Depending on the needs of one's institution, traditional video-editing software products may not be necessary, and all transcoding needs can be met by using only free and open-source software. However, although free and well supported by an active community, software such as FFmpeg comes with its own complications. Many free or open-source software solutions do not have the highly refined and tested graphical user interfaces that people expect in paid solutions, and some solutions, though powerful, are operated through a command-line interface and have no graphical features. As with any array of solutions, one must make compromises when making specifications, as few tools exist at a perfect intersection between functionality and usability. This section takes a closer look at the kinds of software that one might need to capture, transcode, and edit digitized audiovisual resources.

Transcoders

Transcoding software is used to convert digital audiovisual streams from one codec and format to another. The best-known and most robust of this software is FFmpeg, a command-line transcoding program originally developed by programmer Fabrice Bellard and maintained by a cadre of engineers (FFmpeg 2012). FFmpeg incorporates more than one hundred codecs and formats and is capable of transcoding a variety of inputs. Given its robustness and versatility, FFmpeg is often used as an integral supporting component in many popular media players with limited transcoding capabilities, such as VideoLAN's VLC media player and the MPlayer Project's MPlayer media player. While FFmpeg can be used solo to stream and transcode almost any audiovisual media file, it can be a little intimidating to persons with little or no experience with a command-line interface. Furthermore, even to those comfortable using command-line interfaces, such interfaces are not very efficient and are difficult to teach to others. There are many free transcoding programs based on FFmpeg that employ a graphical user interface, or "front end," that will likely be more familiar an experience to the majority of users. A simple Google search of "video transcoders" will yield thousands upon thousands of results, the majority of which will lead you to shareware, freeware, or trialware programs with little or no functionality that often cost upward of $50. The majority of quality transcoders are produced as open-source tools by talented developers and cost nothing to use. It is wise to thoroughly research any software, free or otherwise, before downloading and using.

Transcoding features also exist in all free or licensed video-editing software. One of the most popular such programs, Apple's Final Cut Pro, is capable of transcoding edited videos to a variety of popular modern codecs and formats, such as MP4/H.264 (Apple 2013). Such software is not always necessary in archive and library environments when the goal is simply to transcode raw audiovisual streams into compressed delivery formats. As discussed previously, such tasks can be completed by a variety of free and open-source software. However, the needs of each institution are unique, and all solutions should be considered with regard to technological need, cost, and overall usefulness over time.

Capture Software

All capture systems also require a software program that facilitates communication between a computer's operating system and the capture device, whatever that may be. Depending on the software, such a program will likely allow users to choose the format, bitrate, frame rate, and color space of resultant captures. The options inherent in each program vary, but the aforementioned are basic options generally available in all such programs. There are hundreds of free, open-source, and somewhat suspect capture utilities available for download on the World Wide Web, but like transcoding software, all options under consideration should be thoroughly vetted, tested, and investigated.

Most capture devices, internal or external, are packaged with some form of proprietary capture software. This should be one of the more important considerations when shopping for a capture device, as the software can sometimes dictate the actual usefulness of the device. In some cases, a device is advertised as being able to produce only encoded video, which means that its software will not allow true capture of raw video and resultant files will be compressed. Other devices' software allows users to capture video data in a variety of color spaces and formats and even facilitate compression. It is wise to find the device-software combination that has the greatest number of capture options and allows capture of raw video.

Perhaps the most powerful capture software, free or otherwise, is Audacity, an open-source audio editor designed by programmers at Carnegie Mellon University. Audacity is capable of editing almost any audio file, and with the help of an FFmpeg plug-in, which uses codecs from the aforementioned FFmpeg transcoder, it can export to almost any audio format-codec combination (Audacity Development Team 2012). While robust as an editor, Audacity is most useful as an audio capture program. It can capture in PCM (pulse code modulation) at a maximum of 32 bits and 96 Kbps and interfaces with most known audio capture devices as well as a computer's basic audio inputs (line in). While it captures only audio signals, Audacity is more feature rich and functional a program than many costly audio editors and should be at the top of an institution's list of software to acquire and distribute.

The process of capturing video and audio is a relatively straightforward one compared to the seemingly overwhelming task of making sense of the hundreds of codecs and formats that one can use. It is not enough to simply capture a raw audiovisual signal and distribute it as a gigantic, uncompressed source file. To make it consumable, the file has to be compressed to a fraction of its original size so that it can easily stream from a server to a user or is not too unwieldy to download and view locally. As presented in chapter 2, there are many hundreds of audiovisual codecs and formats, obsolete or in use, which each have unique compression algorithms, are subject to certain technologies, and are not all playable by the same computer or device. The audiovisual engineering and digitization communities have made excellent strides in explaining these formats and their uses, but there are still several competing standards. Audio capture has enjoyed the brunt of these strides given its relative simplicity when compared to video capture, which is more complex, involves more components, and is characterized by far more codecs and formats.

Audio Standards

Over the last decade, the digitization community has made significant progress in setting capture and preservation standards for audio resources. Unlike video capture and preservation, it is fair—and correct—to follow a few assumptions when digitizing and preserving audio resources. For example, audio signals are almost always captured as PCM files, sometimes noted as LPCM (linear pulse code modulation), which the Library of Congress describes as a digital representation of an analog signal. A PCM file is, in effect, a pure and unadulterated digital translation of an audio signal, and it is from PCM files that derivatives are made. Although this is discussed in chapter 2, it is worth mentioning again, as it may be the one universal agreement among members of the audiovisual digitization community. The formats containing PCM are not necessarily as agreed on, and depending on the specific industry, some containers are preferred over others. WAV (Windows Audio File Format) files are well known among PC users and can contain PCM but are not as advanced as other formats, such as BWF (Broadcast Wave Format). The use of one over the other depends on the industry (e.g., broadcast archives vs. academic) and the needs of the specific institution. An argument can be made for preferring older and better-known formats, such as WAV and AIFF (Audio Interchange File Format), as permanent containers for captured audio simply because of their popularity, age, and simplicity. For archival purposes, PCM audio contained in WAV, AIFF, or BWF is preferred.

A Google search for "audio digitization standards" (or some variation thereof) will reveal hundreds of documents from universities, professional organizations, and governmental entities describing their individual standards and practices. It can be an intimidating pursuit to determine which standards to follow, but most such documents share some commonalities. As mentioned earlier, most will recommend PCM as the base representation of analog audio; most will recommend capturing at 96 kHz and a bit depth of 24 bits; finally, most will recommend creating a service or delivery copy as an MP3 or AAC at a bitrate of 192 kbits. Variations in bitrate and sample rate are common. There is some debate as to whether capturing at a sample rate of 96 kHz versus 48 kHz amounts to a detectable difference in quality. Studio recording is typically done at 48 kHz and 24 bits, but many digital preservation organizations, more interested in strict technical quality rather than human-detectable quality, tend to capture at 96 kHz. The debate occurs at the intersection of quality and need: while technically containing more information than a file sampled at 48 kHz, one sampled at 96 kHz will require more hardware resources to process (CPU speed, RAM) and will ultimately be larger.

When researching standards, one should not simply follow what another institution is doing without first asking why it chose the standards that it did and who influenced said standards. There are many authorities on audio engineering that release standards relevant to their own communities as well as others in allied fields. Some trusted authorities follow:

- Audio Engineering Society
- International Association of Sound and Audiovisual Archives
- Association for Recorded Sound Collections
- Federal Agencies Digitization Guidelines Initiative
- National Recording Preservation Board
- Recording Industry Association of America

Many institutions with highly regarded audiovisual digitization standards and guidelines, such as Stanford University (Stanford Media Preservation Lab 2012), and collaborative organizations, such as the Consortium of Academic and Research Libraries in Illinois, maintain standards like those created by the aforementioned professional and government entities. As mentioned previously, these standards are often adaptations, distillations, and conglomerations of a variety of standards with institution-specific wording and capture preferences.

Deciding what deliverables to serve to one's users may be the most troublesome part of selecting and applying standards. MP3 and AAC audio codecs/formats are often preferred, the former because of its popularity and small size relative to quality, the latter for its rising popularity among digital music distributors and overall increase in quality from that represented by MP3. Chapter 2 discusses how there are dozens of audio formats and codecs, each having strengths and weaknesses, but choosing which among these to deliver to one's users must involve some thought. Some institutions provide only one service copy of an audio resource, while others provide several. For example, an institution concerned with interoperability and playability among its users might opt to create a variety of format options, including Ogg Vorbis, MP4/M4A, MP3, and WMA (Windows Media Audio), in hopes of being as inclusive as possible. Other institutions may see fit to serve only that which they have deemed to be the most commonly used format and, perhaps based on user survey, that which is preferred by most users. Serving only one delivery copy can amount to an appreciable surplus in time versus laboring over creating four or five derivatives, but you may not be serving everyone equally.

Video Standards

Unlike audio standards, which enjoy a much higher level of standard development, video is a broader and more complex medium represented by hundreds of different color spaces, formats, and codecs. To further complicate the matter, many videos are paired with audio streams, and one must consider the entire package as one entity. While audio digitization can follow assumptions supported by the sum research of dozens of agencies and hundreds of universities, video is subject to a greater level of variation and debate. In recent years, the Library of Congress (National Digital Information Infrastructure and Preservation Program 2008) and the Society of Motion Picture and Television Engineers (2011) have led the way in setting standards for video capture and preservation and generally recommend audiovisual packages be wrapped in the Materials Exchange Format (MXF), which is a highly advanced platform agnostic container capable of holding a variety of metadata and audiovisual streams. Both organizations recommend said format for archival purposes because of its ability to contain a high number of data and metadata elements, all of which can be referenced in perpetuity and form a complete map of the video. As for the type of codec, there is little consensus.

There are many dozens of video codecs, each being raw, lossy, or losslessly compressed. There is some debate whether captured audiovisual objects should be saved as raw color space (e.g., YUV) within a preferred wrapper or a codec that compresses raw video without losing color information. The advantage to the latter is that the resultant file will be significantly smaller and take up less storage space and be easier to manipulate in editing applications. However, most standards recommend erring on the side of uncompressed capture for archival purposes. If storage space is not a limitation at your institution, it would be wise to keep an uncompressed file for archival purposes and maintain a losslessly compressed version for the purposes of making derivatives or editing.

The Library of Congress has suggested that the lossless compression exhibited by Motion JPEG 2000 makes it the ideal codec for capture. Much research has gone into said codec, but whether it is ideal or not is still being discussed. Perhaps the most relevant fact is that Motion JPEG 2000 is patent encumbered and not readily available in most common video-editing solutions. Free losslessly compressed codecs, such as Huffyuv, Lagarith, and FFV1, are available through popular programs, such as FFmpeg, or as individual codecs that can be configured to work with a variety of capture software. The disadvantage to using any of the aforementioned codecs is that they may not necessarily be usable ten, twenty, or fifty years from now. Raw video, though unwieldy, is more likely to be decipherable in perpetuity.

Among other things, most standards offer some advice on video resolution. If you are operating in North America, your objects will have most likely been recorded on a device following the NTSC (National Television System Committee) analog video standard; thus, your videos will be displayed at a standard 4:3 aspect ratio. This is important to note, as many capture software and transcoding applications will ask for aspect ratio values and/or final video resolution. In the case of standard 4:3 videos, the pixel resolution should be 640 × 480. Increasing the resolution will result in a large frame size when viewed but also reduced definition, as less information is being spread across a larger canvas. Alternatively, reducing resolution will result in a smaller overall file size.

Derivatives, or service copies, are ideally as information rich—visually—as their source files. However, a compressed MP4 (H.264) derived from a 60-GB uncompressed video will still be rather large. Depending on one's streaming capabilities and server infrastructure, serving a 3- or 4-GB file is not a realistic option. In these cases, reducing both the resolution and the bitrate will result in smaller files that can be delivered more easily and faster. As with anything, though, the trade-off is that users will be served a lower-quality video, which may not be universally acceptable.

Perhaps the most important thing to consider when presenting video is how the format will be played—and whether it will be played—in a user's web browser. Like audio files, video objects are not necessarily universally playable. While browsers can be configured to play certain video formats and codecs with the aid of plug-ins, some will not play certain videos, even with the advent of HTML5, which was supposed to have allowed audiovisual playback without regard to platform, plug-in, or browser. For example, browsers such as Apple's Safari and Microsoft's Internet Explorer are not amenable to such open-source formats as Ogg Theora and WebM; Opera, Mozilla Firefox, and Google Chrome browsers are generally supportive of open-source formats but have been known to oppose H.264 video, which is supported in Safari and Internet Explorer. Given the changing landscape of video vis-à-vis support from web browsers, it would be irresponsible to recommend one derivative compression format over another. Given this flux, it would be wise to offer at least three derivative types: MP4 (H.264), Ogg Theora, and MPEG-2, among which most users should be able to find a playable format in their environment.

Ultimately, given the sheer variety of video formats, codecs, and specifications, one should spend some time researching the standards adopted by governments, universities, and other entities, comparing them to one another and to one's own needs. In looking for further advice, the following entities are widely trusted:

- Society of Motion Picture and Television Engineers
- Federal Agencies Digitization Guidelines Initiative
- Society of Broadcast Engineers
- Library of Congress Audio-Visual Conservation Division/Packard Campus

Sample Digitization Workflows

To illustrate the components and processes in an audiovisual digitization program, this section provides two basic and extensible workflows: one for an audio-only capture process, the other for an audiovisual. Assumptions are made with regard to equipment and software but are noted before each workflow.

Audio-Only Workflow

The workflow herein details the processes typical of digitizing an audio resource. The following assumptions are made:

- User has a basic audiocassette deck with standard RCA stereo outputs and auto-reverse.
- User has a PC running the latest version of Microsoft Windows operating system and a working 3.5-mm LINE IN input.
- User has Audacity audio-editing software installed on PC.
- User has an male-to-male cable: RCA stereo to 3.5-mm stereo.
- User is digitizing one two-sided audiocassette tape.
- User has headphones with a quarter-inch connector or quarter-inch connector adaptor.

Step 1: Prepare Equipment

1. Situate audiocassette deck near PC.
2. Plug in audiocassette deck.

3. Connect RCA-to-3.5-mm stereo cable (RCA end) to audiocassette deck's STEREO OUT (labels vary).
4. Connect RCA-to-3.5-mm stereo cable (3.5-mm end) to PC's LINE IN (labels vary).

Step 2: Record

1. Turn on audiocassette deck.
2. Insert audiocassette that you wish to capture.
3. Connect headphones to audiocassette deck's PHONE jack (labels vary).
4. Play audiocassette, listening through headphones to assess quality.
5. Once satisfied, rewind tape to beginning and disconnect headphones.
6. Launch Audacity.
   a. Select input device (sound card).
   b. Choose sample rate.
   c. Begin recording.
7. After Audacity has been recording dead air for a few seconds, begin playback of the audiocassette.
   a. Recording input will be indicated in Audacity via the left and/or right channel meter.
8. When playback ceases, you have two options:
   a. continue recording while the tape reverses to play back its other side, or
   b. end recording and begin a new track for the tape's opposite side.
9. Once finished recording, you may edit the track (or tracks) or continue to step 3.

Step 3: Make Derivatives

1. Save/export the recorded material as PCM/LPCM in either a WAV or AIFF container.
2. Derivatives can be made at this point with any of the following formats/codecs (depending on add-ons and plug-ins):
   a. Ogg Vorbis
   b. MP3
   c. AAC (MP4/M4A)
   d. WMA

Audiovisual Workflow

The workflow herein details the processes typical of digitizing an audiovisual resource. The following assumptions are made:

- User has an S-VHS VCR with S-Video and RCA outputs.
- User has a PC running the latest version of Microsoft Windows operating system.
- User has a PCI capture card with RCA and S-Video inputs installed in the PC.
- User has VirtualDub video capture software installed on the PC.
- User has FFmpeg or a transcoder utilizing FFmpeg.
- User has one S-Video cable with two male ends.
- User has one set of RCA cables (red and white) with two male ends.

Step 1: Prepare Equipment

1. Situate VCR near PC.
2. Plug in VCR.
3. Connect one end of S-Video cable to VCR's S-Video OUT (labels vary); connect other end to capture card's S-Video IN (labels vary).
4. Connect one set of ends of RCA cable (red and white) to VCR's AUDIO OUT's (labels vary); connect the other set of ends to the capture card's AUDIO IN's (labels vary).

Step 2: Record

1. Turn on VCR.
2. Launch VirtualDub.
   a. Select video capture device.
3. Insert videocassette into VCR and begin playback.
   a. Review tape's contents, viewing through VirtualDub to assess quality.
   b. Once satisfied, rewind tape to beginning.
4. In VirtualDub, specify color space/codec for output (AVI is only option for container).
5. Begin capturing blank signal.
6. After a few seconds, begin playback of tape in VCR.
7. Once video has reached its end, cease recording.
8. Save/export the captured video.
   a. If editing is required, make a second copy, naming it differently and using it for editing and derivation creation.

Step 3: Make Derivatives

1. Launch FFmpeg or FFmpeg-based transcoder.
   a. Open AVI of captured video.
   b. Create derivatives as needed, including but not limited to
      i. MP4/MOV (H.264 video and AAC audio)
      ii. MPEG-2 TS (MPEG-2 video and MP3 audio)
      iii. Ogg (Theora video and Vorbis audio)

ⓖ Key Points

There is far too much to be written on the subject of digitizing audiovisual materials for libraries, but despite innumerable differences between institutions' requirements and capabilities, the key concepts remain identical:

- Understand technological strengths and weaknesses, and use this knowledge to come to strike a balance between cost and control.
- When engaging a digitization vendor, never be fearful of asking as many questions as possible.
- When digitizing in-house, be prepared to make significant investments in both equipment and labor, and never assume that the former comes without the latter.

- There is no need to attain an expert-level grasp of audiovisual technology, but a topical understanding of capture equipment, media, software, and connectors and how they work together is essential.
- Documentation of workflows, standards, and other processes is essential in completing an effective and efficient digitization project, as well as making it easier for the progression of later projects.

Once a solid technological foundation is set, digitization workflows devised, and standards applied, a project team will be able to easily address the presentation of resources. Simply digitizing objects is typically not enough to constitute a digital initiative, although it can be in cases were materials are captured purely for archival purposes. In most cases, however, content must be delivered to users in some fashion. The extent to which the material should be accessible, the options for content delivery, and a real-world case study compose the following chapter, which is intended as a basic primer to selecting tools for making audiovisual content accessible to select or wide audiences.

References

Apple. 2013. "Final Cut Pro X Technical Specifications." http://www.apple.com/finalcutpro/specs/.

Audacity Development Team. 2013. "About Audacity." http://audacity.sourceforge.net/about/credits.

CARLI Digital Collections Users' Group, Standards Subcommittee. 2010. "Guidelines for the Creation of Digital Collections: Digitization Best Practices for Moving Images." Consortium of Academic Research Libraries in Illinois. http://www.carli.illinois.edu/sites/files/digital_collections/documentation/guidelines_for_audio.pdf.

FFmpeg. 2012. "FFmpeg Legal." http://www.ffmpeg.org/legal.html.

National Digital Information Infrastructure and Preservation Program. 2008. "Linear Pulse Code Modulated Audio (LPCM)." U.S. Library of Congress. http://www.digitalpreservation.gov/formats/fdd/fdd000011.shtml.

Society of Motion Picture and Television Engineers. 2011. "Standards Facilitate Interoperability." https://www.smpte.org/standards.

Stanford Media Preservation Lab. 2012. "Audio Digitization Services at SMPL." http://lib.stanford.edu/stanford-media-preservation-lab/audio-digitization.

Texas Commission on the Arts. 2004. "Videotape Identification and Assessment Guide." http://www.arts.texas.gov/wp-content/uploads/2012/04/video.pdf.

University of Michigan. n.d. "Vendors for Audio Digitization and Preservation." http://www.lib.umich.edu/files/audio_digitization_services.pdf.

Presentation and Access

◎ Preservation and Access Basics

Digitizing audiovisual materials effectively and faithfully is a major victory in the work of any digitalist or librarian. There are so many steps and processes involved in simply making the analog digital—and doing it at a minimum of cost and loss of material fidelity. But merely turning an audiocassette tape into a WAV file and storing it somewhere is not enough: for a project to be successful, well used, and worth the effort, that WAV file must be widely accessible. Many audiovisual materials are digitized purely as a preservative measure and, due to copyright issues, cannot be made publicly available; however, the majority of digitization efforts require provision of access. Even such videos or audios that cannot be granted to an interested public might still be candidates for controlled access by select groups. The concern of this chapter is twofold: first, the provision of access to the general public or predetermined sets of person; second, the way to accomplish such access in a meaningful, equitable, and productive way.

Access can be granted in a variety of ways—through a web-based platform (e.g., a digital repository), a highly specialized streaming media system, or controlled on-site delivery. This chapter discusses the differences between technologies for hosting and delivering (providing files or content) to users and considerations for selecting the appropriate system. Among the most important considerations are

- Desired qualities
- Legal condition of resources
- Technology

Once fully addressed, these considerations will inform any decision made to acquire a specific streaming media solution—or, perhaps, in the decision to avoid streaming media solutions altogether. These criteria and considerations are congealed into a real-world case study on the selection of a streaming media system.

⊚ Qualities of Streaming Media Systems

Like any other tool or software, streaming media systems or generic platforms for hosting audiovisual resources can be ideal, close to ideal, or too far from the ideal to even be considered. To determine the needed tool, librarians and archivists must establish a list of basic requirements or qualities that they desire for whatever tool they acquire. Libraries will have different needs based on constituencies, budget, and other factors, but there are basic qualities that every librarian should strive to find in a system, qualities that are specific to archives and libraries not found in commercial-grade or enterprise solutions. The challenge lies in finding a product or service that exists at the crossroads of affordability and quality, as is the case with most purchasable things, but it is a realistic expectation to favor compromise over abandonment when looking for the right tool.

The basic qualities of a library-specific streaming media system should consist of the following:

Library-specific metadata: Commercial systems or enterprise solutions in streaming media and content management rarely, if ever, accommodate common library metadata schema such as MARC, Dublin Core, or MODS. A person should not expect such accommodations from businesses that provide general-use software or are geared toward the corporate world, but there are solutions that can at least provide generic schema that can be shaped in the image of Dublin Core or MODS. This is an area where librarians will need to be comfortable making a compromise. There are currently no fully developed solutions aimed directly at libraries.

Authentication: Most commercial or academic systems are capable of integrating with a client's directory protocol (e.g., LDAP) so that users entering the system can be authenticated as permitted entrants. This is useful when curating and hosting content such as licensed videos or copyright material for which administrators may only provide access to, for instance, students and faculty. A similarly acceptable quality would be a system's ability to provide IP filtering so that only users attempting to access content within an institution's unique IP range are granted access. Alongside proxy control, which forces users trying to use a streaming media system to enter through an institution's unique filtering system, IP filtering is less common—and desirable—than directory authentication.

Integration with other systems: As libraries and archives expand their roles to offer resources and services through course and learning management systems such as

Blackboard and Moodle, they should strive to find a platform compatible with their institution's current software. The ability to deliver audiovisual content to specific courses through the integration of two technologies, such as a streaming media system and a learning management system, will go a long way in strengthening a library's role as a knowledge provider. The ability to interface with course and learning management systems is currently a standard feature of commercial and enterprise streaming solutions.

Transcoding: With the saturation of digital video has come the proliferation of dozens of formats and decoding standards. As standards change, interoperability between old and new becomes an issue and can cause accessibility issues. Transcoding, the process by which multimedia are transformed from one format and codec to another, is an essential component of any streaming media system. The process essentially standardizes all uploaded video, regardless of its original format, so that nearly anyone can view and replay content.

Preservation: The issue of preservation, which is concerned with the long-term safekeeping of materials and their migration from unusable to usable formats, is a difficult one to address. There is handful of software that can manage the stewardship of digital objects (e.g., Ex Libris's Rosetta or DuraSpace's DuraCloud), but tools specifically for the preservation of audiovisual objects are few and far between. Unlike PDFs or word-processing documents, for example, video is extraordinarily complex and space-consumptive and can pose problems for long-term maintenance. Like metadata, forgiving the lack of a preservation component in a streaming media system may be a necessary concession.

Platform agnostic: Users are not necessarily going to be using a library's streaming media system on a PC or Mac within the walls of a library or archive. There is just as good of a chance that users will be accessing resources via mobile phones, tablets, and other devices through several different browsers. Whatever tool a librarian chooses, it absolutely must be accessible, and a system dependent on too many technological assumptions will cripple a library's usefulness.

No or high limits on uploading or storage: Open-source solutions managed in-house will be limited only by local storage space or cloud subscriptions, but many streaming systems that offer hosting, free or subscription based, will have some limitation of the size of each file uploaded, as well as overall space limits. Ideally, an archivist should find a solution with no limits on file uploads or storage, but the ideal is not always attainable and, in the case of hosted solutions, is quite rare. It is more realistic to expect to pay for storage space, but unless there is an immediate need for hundreds of terabytes, costs are generally low and reasonable.

There are certainly other qualities not listed that might be desirable in a streaming media system, but the aforementioned are generally going to satisfy core users. In any case, the persons tasked with finding the "right" system should spend as much time as possible polling potential users for their input and making a set list of "musts" for a system. There are dozens of services and software that a team can explore and try to assess whether any match desired qualities. It is wise to conduct a trial on as many solutions as possible and record detailed data on how each system met—or did not meet—the desired qualifications.

The legal conditions of a resource are the circumstances surrounding its creation, as well as the current status of its copyright. To pursue a streaming media system or related service, a librarian must understand the legal accessibility of his or her materials. If such things are assumed and not fully explored, a librarian and an institution could find themselves in quite a bit of trouble. The only thing that a person should assume about an object's legal accessibility is that it is ambiguous and needs clarification.

Something that is in copyright cannot necessarily be streamed to the general public. Copyrighted materials, such as documentaries on VHS or music CDs, are covered under U.S. copyright law and cannot simply be uploaded for all to see or hear. There are cases wherein copyright has been relinquished, abandoned, or transferred and a librarian may, after fulfilling due diligence in determining the current state of an object's copyright, upload and make available that object. Videos and audios sometimes do fall out of copyright, leaving it up to the librarian or archivist to interpret the object's condition and make a sound judgment based on whatever evidence is available.

It may seem obvious that someone intent on digitizing a circulating VHS collection to make it accessible to modern users will encounter many copyright roadblocks. While this is true, it is still worth the time and effort to verify that rights can or cannot be acquired. The value of a VHS collection trapped in its own antiquity is likely very high, and most potential users today will not be able to easily make use of such media. Likewise, it should not be assumed that archival media, such as old reel-to-reel audiotapes or other material never produced for profit, are exempt from copyright. If a work was created by an individual or group entity, then it is likely governed to some extent by copyright law. The difference between archival materials and commercial content is the ease with which rights can be acquired and the level of use typically allowed.

For archival materials, rights to digitize and host publicly may have already been acquired as part of the original donation or deposition. If arrangements were never made, as in the case of materials given to an archive or library before the existence of the Internet or the notion of digitization, acquiring permission may be more difficult. Many libraries assume rights because of ownership, as in that which is granted by a deed of gift, but it is always best to ask the original owner if digitization and public hosting are acceptable. If the original donor and his or her relatives or surrogates cannot be found or contacted, due diligence should be documented in the event that a complaint is lodged.

For commercially produced videos and films, it is absolutely necessary to contact both the distributor and the publisher of the material to ask for third-party distribution rights. Many companies are familiar with such requests from libraries, especially regarding videos on VHS for which no modern equivalent can be purchased. If a company grants permission to digitize and host material, it is likely certain that restrictions will be requested, such as allowing only one authenticated user at a time to watch a streamed version of a video or perhaps allowing for only one DVD copy to be produced, which will still create accessibility where there previously was none. Ultimately, the onus of permission identification is on librarians and archivists, and it is their responsibility to make certain that all materials they digitize and host—publicly or behind usage restrictions—are permitted in such a state (copyright is explored more deeply in chapter 4; for student-created content, see textbox 6.1).

PROJECT STARTERS: STUDENT AUDIOVISUAL MATERIALS

Description

Students at a college or university are some of the most prolific producers of intellectual and creative content. Often, their efforts are reviewed for grades or as part of a thesis or capstone project, then discarded or forgotten. Many universities maintain loosely organized archives of student-submitted materials, but rarely are such archives searchable or usable. These archives can include anything from student films made for a single course or entire portfolios of work submitted as part of a terminal degree project. Many academic entities also record student projects, such as pin-ups for an architecture program or undergraduate research seminars. These resources certainly exist, so the biggest problem facing archivists and librarians interested in crafting a project is actually finding and acquiring the materials.

Common Sources

- University archives
- Academic departments—art and media programs, architecture schools, journalism departments
- University news and public affairs units
- Student-run television news programs
- Student organizations
- Fraternal and sororal organizations

Common Physical and Digital Formats

- VHS videocassettes
- Standard audiocassette tapes
- DVDs
- CDs
- MPEG-2 video
- MPEG-4 video and audio
- MP3 audio

Digitization Hurdles

- Permission acquisition from students who may no longer be associated with university or college
- Actually finding the materials
- Vetting material for appropriateness

(Continued)

Presentation and Access Technologies

A project team can pursue many technologies that will provide meaningful access to digitized audiovisual resources, so the challenge is not in finding a tool but in deciding among dozens. Before a specific product or service is selected, though, a librarian must decide the type of technology that she or he wants to employ in the presentation of resources. There are free, popular resources, such as YouTube and Vimeo; subscription-based digital repository software; and hybrid open-source systems, such as Kaltura, which can be run locally and configured independently or subscribed to via a cloud-based service. Each type of system (popular, subscription, open source) provides unique opportunities and considerable challenges. It is not uncommon for one institution to invest in a variety of systems complementing one another.

Popular Platforms

Many video-hosting and sharing services are freely available (or at a nominal fee depending on usage) via the Internet. These services are considered popular because of their generalized features and audiences, as well as their lean toward entertainment-oriented content. These facts should not be considered detriments, though, as such systems can help popularize even seemingly mundane digital resources. They are also effective at reaching far-flung users that may not have access to highly specialized systems. The following capsules discuss the three most popular web-based media-hosting services and compare their strengths and weaknesses relative to common library audiovisual resources.

YouTube

To say that YouTube is popular is a crushing understatement. Its centrality to the world of video sharing, hosting, and media dispersal is largely unchallenged. YouTube is a free web-based service that allows users to upload videos, effectively without limit, and view those uploaded by others. The only restrictions exist in the ownership of content: users must own what they upload (i.e., created the content or acquired it legally); otherwise, they could be in breach of dozens of copyright laws. For example, a user cannot simply upload an episode of a popular television show or even a music video. YouTube employs algorithmic software that trawls its servers in search of copyrighted content, able to discern music owned by a record company from the background of a home video or detect copyrighted video streams. While the copyright-enforcement software deployed by YouTube may seem daunting, it can be disputed in the case of errors or misjudgments, especially where academic institutions are involved.

YouTube's strengths lie in its ability to quickly disseminate a large amount of data to a high number of individuals (see textbox 6.2). A video's size or length is hardly ever an issue, as Google (YouTube's owner) provides nearly unlimited storage space for users, which is a common concern with locally run or subscription-based services. Videos can be edited after upload with a few simple tools, and basic metadata, such as descriptions, geographic coordinates, and genre/subject, can be added. Videos in YouTube can be curated fairly easily by using the playlist function, which lets users assemble sets of videos into ordered arrangements of content shareable through direct linking or embedding. It is arguable whether the playlist function is really curatorial, as it depends on assumed context or, more so, the will of the user, who can choose whether to read the provided descriptions or not.

Perhaps the biggest drawbacks to using YouTube are its inability to allow restricted use of content based on IP or local authority and its popularity (see textbox 6.3). The former relates to some libraries' need to provide access to certain materials to a select group based on IP ranges or a server-based authority system. YouTube cannot facilitate such restriction; it only allows users to make videos unlisted, which prevents them from being revealed in search results, or entirely private, revealed to as many as fifty individuals of the user's choosing (YouTube 2013). The latter issue, that of popularity, seems

---

TEXTBOX 6.2.

YOUTUBE'S STRENGTHS

Popular: YouTube is unmatched in popularity and will likely reach the widest audience of any technology in its class.

Familiarity: Due to its wide use, YouTube is familiar to millions of people. Such familiarity reduces the learning curve and can attract users.

Indexing: Owned by Google, YouTube is quickly indexed in the world's most popular search engine and available to researchers nearly immediately.

No cost: YouTube does not levy fees or maintain echelons of service—all users are effectively equal in terms of capability.

like something intrinsically positive. While it is true that popularity of a product such as YouTube widens possible user bases and effectively self-promotes by osmosis, popularity comes with a price. Among the downsides are belligerent commenters, sudden and unforeseen copyright issues (perhaps an archival video inadvertently contains a few seconds of a copyrighted song), advertising, and lack of control over the look and feel of a landing page. Advertisements may preempt videos that contain disputed content, although advertisements on the same page as a video, like those found on sidebars, can be disabled.

Vimeo

Similar to YouTube, Vimeo is a popular web-based service for video hosting and sharing. Unlike YouTube, however, Vimeo has a definite lean toward educational content, art, and documentary. This is not to say that YouTube does not contain such things. Rather, Vimeo has an aversion to advertising: it is visible only to users with free accounts and without the same level of saturation found on YouTube. Vimeo has many strengths and weaknesses in its own right, but comparisons to YouTube are unavoidable.

Among Vimeo's strengths is its promotion of high-quality content from artists, designers, and filmmakers (see textbox 6.4). Because of Vimeo's emphasis on high-definition video, many creative individuals gravitate toward the service to ensure proper representation of their content. This level of quality may not be a necessity for librarians, though, as the majority of archival videos converted from analog to digital formats will not benefit from high-definition conversion. Born-digital content created over the last few years, such as student art projects or departmental education videos, or other materials that are being preemptively archived will certainly be strong candidates for Vimeo. Alongside the adherence to high-quality content, Vimeo has a particularly elegant site design that is more conducive to curation than YouTube's. Despite its relative aesthetic maturity, Vimeo is still not wholly customizable as would be an in-house solution. However, as with YouTube, videos can be embedded in a website or content management system to simulate the effect of an in-house hosting platform.

Many of these features come at a price, though, and a literal one at that (see textbox 6.5). While YouTube does not charge users for unfettered uploading of content to its platform, Vimeo has severe restrictions on user abilities. For example, persons with free accounts are limited to 500 MB per week of upload space, a single channel (like YouTube's playlist feature), and one high-definition-video upload per week. Individuals who opt to increase their abilities need to pay for a "Plus" account, which allows up to 5 GB of uploads per week, unlimited high-definition videos, and, perhaps best of all, no advertising (Vimeo 2013). These logistical restraints and the need to pay to remove them might be enough to dissuade an educational institution from pursuing Vimeo. Granted, Plus accounts are, at the time of writing, $9.95 per month, but not every archivist is willing to pay for a service when a similar one (YouTube) is available at no financial cost with practically no restraints on usage.

Internet Archive

Internet Archive (IA) is not a dedicated video-hosting platform but a free (and free to use) digital library accessible to anyone. It hosts content from thousands of educational institutions and even more individuals. Like YouTube and Vimeo, IA allows users to upload videos, add metadata, and disseminate content through direct linking, embedding, and availability in search engines. Unlike YouTube and Vimeo, though, IA has an explicit cultural and historical directive, which is to provide free and unfettered access to the accumulated digitized knowledge of the world. Digitized knowledge, in the case of IA, extends from archived websites to rare books to archival oral histories and ephemeral films.

Among IA's many strengths is its robust system for accepting, hosting, and deriving audiovisual materials (see textbox 6.6). IA's derivation system is helpful for archivists that want to upload a video and have it automatically derived into several formats, including OGG, MPEG4, MPEG1, MPEG2, and RealMedia, all at various sizes and bitrates. Videos and audio files can then be described with a handful of stock metadata, including title, creator, and description, as well as an unlimited number of user-determined metadata. This feature more closely simulates the kind of metadata schema to which librarians and archivists are most familiar (e.g., Dublin Core, MARC). Videos and audio files uploaded are given dedicated pages within a collection, although novel collections can be created only once a user has reached a fifty-page requirement. Until that time, all uploaded content is stored in a generic collection called Community Video. In either case, whether in the generic collection or a novel one, all videos and audios behave identically, with options to embed, share, and describe.

Once a user has reached the fifty-page requirement to build a dedicated collection, he or she will be able to add a collection description, institutional logo, and manage content. This new collection will be moved to an appropriate top-level collection where it can be browsed as a unique set of materials (IA 2013). IA's biggest detriment is the limitation on collection creation and the need to upload a certain number of items to be given access to collection tools (see textbox 6.7). Many archivists will want total control over their resources and how they are presented to the world, but IA can offer only so much. As is discussed in chapter 7, IA is often used as a secondary platform for hosting content for purposes of promotion and saturation or, in some cases, as a free repository to which users can point through in-house content management systems.

Vimeo, YouTube, and IA all have their places in a librarian's toolkit, but they are not able to offer the same level of control that a librarian may have come to expect from digital repositories. Users of platforms such as Ex Libris's DigiTool or OCLC's ContentDM will be averse to using systems that offer little in the way of customization and distribution control and may look to such popular video-hosting services as ways to augment and promote collections held in repositories more highly tailored to the needs of libraries and archives.

Streaming Media Platforms

Streaming media platforms are technologies designed to stream media to users through the Internet. Where they differ from popular web-based platforms is in their customizability and intent, which is typically aimed at educational institutions and corporations. Many such systems can be purchased like any other software, subscribed to like a SaaS (software as a service), or acquired as an open-source package. There are many advantages to using a dedicated streaming media platform, but most are tempered by high financial costs or the necessity for expert programming and web development support. Adoption of streaming media systems in libraries has been slow. The corporate and entertainment worlds, however, have been particularly supportive of such technologies. The following capsules discuss the strengths and weaknesses of one common streaming media platform with wide appeal and one system designed specifically for academic libraries.

Kaltura

Kaltura is arguably the most popular streaming media platform on the market today (see textbox 6.8). It is capable of managing and serving audiovisual content to users on the Internet, through mobile devices, or in customized environments. Unlike a lot of similar solutions, Kaltura offers its software as an open-source package, which can be altered and improved by users who are allowed to integrate it with other technologies to fit their unique needs.

Despite its weaknesses, Kaltura is popular for a reason: it is able to satisfy an array of requirements shared by various institutions, and if the necessity for authenticated, curated, and programmatically extensible streaming media is an administrative mission, Kaltura is currently the most complete solution (see textbox 6.9). More information on Kaltura, its development, and features can be found at http://www.kaltura.org or http://corp.kaltura.com.

Avalon Media System

Avalon Media System (AVS) is currently being developed by technologists at Indiana University and Northwestern University as part of a series of Institute of Museum and Library Services grants. The aim of AVS is to provide libraries and archives a highly specialized and open-source media management and streaming system. AVS is currently in beta, its first release (AVS 1.0) having been issued for trial in mid-2013, with further releases planned between the end of 2013 and throughout 2014. While the system, as

TEXTBOX 6.8.

KALTURA'S STRENGTHS

Open source: can be altered and improved on a programmatic level.

Transcoding: converts uploaded media from one format to another.

Authentication: allows users to integrate platform into local authentication system to deliver video to select groups securely and legally.

Adaptive streaming: delivers audiovisual content to different devices with varying connections in such a way that behooves each user.

Integration: can be configured to interact with a variety of popular learning management systems, such as Blackboard and Sakai, as well as content management systems, such as WordPress and Drupal.

Levels of Service

SaaS: paid software as a service whereby Kaltura manages all technical aspects of the platform leaving content management to the user.

On-prem: paid on-premises solution whereby Kaltura's platform is hosted locally by the user but supported by Kaltura.

Community: free open-source version of Kaltura where users download, configure, and host all aspects of the software with no paid support from Kaltura.

TEXTBOX 6.9.

KALTURA'S WEAKNESSES

Cost: The hosted or on-premises versions of Kaltura require a significant initial investment as well as ongoing annual payments that may be too great for some institutions.

Labor: If users are unable to pay for the hosted versions of Kaltura and want to pursue the open-source solution, they will still need to invest in programmers, web developers/designers, and general IT support to configure and maintain the platform. While many institutions already have such support, librarians and administrators must decide whether their IT professionals can spare the time necessary to maintain an intensive solution such as Kaltura.

Not library-centric: Kaltura is a broad solution capable of fulfilling the needs of a variety of user types, but academic libraries will be hard-pressed to find the ideal nexus of cost, ease of use, and adherence to library-specific metadata and control schema.

TEXTBOX 6.10.

AVALON MEDIA SYSTEM'S STRENGTHS

Library centricity: has support for library-type metadata schema, integration with course management systems, and authentication.

Consists of other open-source technology: is built with media capture and streaming tools from Opencast Matterhorn and the increasingly popular Hyrda development framework.

Open source: can be modified, altered, and tailored to fit the needs of a variety of institutions.

Faceted searches and browsing: allows users to browse or search on the basis of facets rather than just text.

Preservation: unlike other media streaming systems, will be able to integrate directly with various data preservation technologies based on popular schema.

of this writing, is only in beta and hardly represents the total of the development team's work, it is a promising solution for libraries and archives struggling to find the best platform for noncommercial content (see textbox 6.10).

While the current weakness of not being fully developed is a large one (see textbox 6.11), AVS has promise. Being developed by individuals in the academic library world, AVS will eventually be able to offer a level of specificity not offered by most other services. It is forgivable to eschew such a solution, though, as a system may be required as soon as possible and the wait for a possibly ideal solution may not be desirable. For some institutions, the wait may be worth the delay in offering a streaming service, but investments in such technologies should not be taken lightly. More information on AVS and its development can be found at http://www.avalonmediasystem.org.

Discussion

The selection of a technology is dependent on more factors than those described in this chapter. It is common that commitments to current technologies, especially to those that

TEXTBOX 6.11.

AVALON MEDIA SYSTEM'S WEAKNESSES

Not fully developed: is still being developed and cannot necessarily fully deliver on each of its features as a beta release.

No hosted version: is much like the strictly self-hosted, open-source version of Kaltura in that it relies on the wherewithal and skills of each customer; may be a problem for potential users who like its features but lack the IT infrastructure and support necessary for a self-hosted system.

are subscription based, can prevent a librarian from moving forward with a newfound—and ideal—solution. In such situations, it is best to make clean breaks when possible and be patient. More difficult to abandon than technologies are commitments made to consortia. To defray the cost of expensive technologies such as digital repositories or streaming media systems, libraries band to make use of a single system at lower individual costs. If, for example, it turns out that the staff and faculty at one library become dissatisfied with a consortial technology and wish to abandon it in favor of something else, they may not necessarily be able to make a clean break. Simply leaving a consortial commitment could increase the financial burden on the other institutions in the consortium and prove a political misstep.

There is no need to labor on with a technology that is not useful or satisfying, though. Timing, honesty, and political deftness are key in withdrawing from a consortial commitment. One tactic is to discuss openly the shortcomings of the current technology and how the preferred solution makes up for them. This conversation should also include a discussion on how the current technology can be updated or altered to compensate for its failings. Finally, a library's administrators should offer access to a trial environment of any new technologies being considered to members of the consortium; that way, the possibility for further collaboration under a new system will arise.

⊚ Case Study

The following case study features the librarians and technologists at the Auraria Library in Denver, Colorado, a tri-institutional library serving the University of Colorado Denver, Metropolitan State University of Denver, and Community College of Denver. Auraria Library was faced with the need for a technology to facilitate the secure streaming of copyrighted content to staff, students, and faculty at three institutions. While a more complex scenario than most—and likely unique due to the library's constituency—this case study delves into the many things that can go right and wrong with the selection of a streaming media system and, ultimately, how one is selected and assessed. The system selected—which is referred to as Technology A (TA) for the purposes of this study—was ultimately abandoned in favor of another solution, but the reasons therein are multifaceted and not disparaging of the former system.

In late 2012, faculty and staff at Auraria Library noticed a need for a streaming media system capable of delivering content to several thousand users. The need arose from the observation that many faculty and students were frequently requesting the digitization of VHS tapes—documentaries mostly—for use in classrooms and assignments. Without the capabilities to digitize and securely host videos, Auraria's librarians could not provide wide and simple access to thousands of hours of content on obsolete media. It became clear that something needed to be done to satisfy the growing demand of the library's user base. Without the aid of a streaming media system, Auraria's librarians identified the following core issues:

Access: Tapes cannot be checked out for external use, and only a few VHS players are available for use.

Copyright: Making digital versions of VHS tapes is technologically feasible but not necessarily legal.

Decay: VHS tapes degrade over time and, unless copied or digitized and migrated regularly, will eventually be unusable.

Obsolescence: The majority of VHS tapes in the collection can no longer be obtained in modern formats, and secondary VHS copies are simply not attainable.

To address these issues, librarians at Auraria decided that any solution other than a streaming media system would be problematic. First, abandoning the VHS tapes would be a dereliction of a librarian's duty to constituents. Second, a straightforward solution, such as the purchase of more VHS players, would not really aid in access and would simply create more dependence on a dead medium. Finally, simple ignorance of the afore-mentioned issues would create an access vacuum, one that might be filled by another in-stitution or a solution not provided by Auraria. Given the content to be streamed, libraries at Auraria came to the conclusion that a popular solution, such as YouTube, would not be appropriate. As discussed earlier in this chapter, copyrighted content cannot simply be put on YouTube or any other provider. But copyright was not the only hurdle. The librarians needed a system that could provide access to unlimited users, transcode video into a standard platform-agnostic format, and offer a hosted solution that required little on-site maintenance or support other than content curation.

The following features were determined to be necessary in a streaming solution for Auraria Library:

Authentication: clears users for use of a video or resource by authenticating against an authority system.

Transcoding: the ability to ingest (nearly) any format and deliver it to users in another format, preferably a standard one with a high chance for end user playability.

Hosting: the ability of a system's creators to provide file and database hosting on remote servers, relieving the subscribing entity of most on-site maintenance obligations.

With those three basic features, Auraria's administrators sought out solutions. After consulting with staff at the three colleges served by Auraria Library, administrators and staff determined that a small-scale collaborative solution with a few local partners within the University of Colorado Denver would be best. After investigating several systems, Auraria selected TA, making a yearlong trial commitment with the option to extend.

Content selection was fairly straightforward, and instruction and research librarians at Auraria decided to pursue a VHS digitization pilot. One hundred of the most com-monly requested VHS tapes were entered into a list and their publishers and/or distribu-tors contacted. The project team responsible for contacting supposed rights holders were charged simply with asking a few basic questions:

- Is tape *X* available as a DVD or digital download?
- If tape *X* is not available in a modern format, may Auraria Library digitize and host it on a protected streaming system?
- If streaming of tape *X* is now allowed, can Auraria Library make a single DVD copy of the tape and make it available to students, faculty, and staff?

Permission to digitize and host VHS tapes was permitted in most cases, with only a handful of publishers unavailable for contact. In such cases, where the copyright holder could be contacted, due diligence in permission acquisition was documented and the tape slated for migration to a modern format. A trusted audiovisual digitization vendor was contacted to digitize a sampling of thirty tapes as well as create a single DVD copy of each title. Digitization was successful and the digital versions uploaded to the newly implemented TA.

The success of digitizing and hosting a smattering of VHS tapes was tempered by a series of technological and bibliographic issues encountered by librarians and IT staff. While the three basic features requested by Auraria were essentially delivered, the project implementation team realized that it had not asked enough questions and accounted for future problems. The failings were not just those of the system but Auraria as well.

Problems

First among the issues with TA was authentication, which is typically a simple thing. However, in the case of an academic library serving three separate schools with unique authentication structures, a simple thing became highly complicated. To authenticate users, Auraria had become accustomed to the use of an integrated library system that issued a unique, library-specific identity to each student, regardless of his or her institutional affiliation. This was not compatible with TA, which preferred the use of lightweight directory access protocol or similar systems that draw usernames and credentials from a general campus directory. This hurdle was temporarily surmounted by the creation of a proxy-enabled URL that would redirect TA's users to a separate log-in page based on the integrated library system. This solution was more of an ad hoc fix, however, and proved to be unreliable.

As more and more content was being uploaded to TA, curators began to notice that transcoding was not always successful and that some videos needed to be uploaded several times before they were finally transcoded. A solution to this issue was never offered by TA or discovered by Auraria's librarians, and the issue itself proved to be a tremendous time-sink. Compounding the upload problems, curators became frustrated with TA's lack of metadata. As mentioned earlier in this chapter, many streaming media systems do not offer library-specific metadata schema and are averse to altering core features. TA's metadata was fairly generic and not extensible, but this was less a failing of the system and more one of Auraria's. Had the project team accounted for metadata input methods and made it a requirement of a system to have library-specific metadata, TA would likely never have been selected. Furthermore, due to TA's lean toward corporate environments and primary and secondary education, a change could not have been expected based on the complaint of one subscriber.

Finally, and perhaps most important, Auraria failed to select a solution at the crux of value and cost. TA's cost was very high, even when compared with similar technologies, but its value to Auraria was ultimately low. While TA was capable of hosting PDFs, e-books, and other media that require authentication, it did so spartanly without many options for improvement. Auraria's collection managers realized that a solution aimed solely at the authenticated hosting of obsolete VHS tapes was not worth the high cost. It became clear that a library-specific solution was needed that was not purely for the hosting of video, something that was extensible and integrable. To make the situation even clearer, the local partners who had originally invested in TA were beginning to back out, fearing its usability on a large scale in the face of its many problems.

Lessons

After repeated attempts to find a solution to the previously mentioned problems that would not necessitate withdrawal, Auraria Library's administrators abandoned TA. Despite the financial costs and effort put into trying to make TA work for Auraria, the experience was ultimately instructive. Several lessons were learned about selecting a streaming media system, out of which grew a more concerted and much deeper discussion about requirements and long-term usability. Among these lessons are the following:

- When engaging a system's creators, ask questions of functionality specific to the institution, not just in a general sense. Doing so will ensure that a system's features in the context of a specific institution will truly apply.
- Look for a solution that has multiple uses beyond those required by the institution. Considering this is akin to planning for the future rather than the present.
- Discuss solutions with potential users such as faculty, as they may have valuable input on the kinds of things that they require out of a streaming media solution.
- During a trial or evaluative period of a product, make a point to stress-test it; taking the system to its limits is the only way to find possible problems that might not otherwise arise.
- Never assume anything.

A solution was eventually selected that had buy-in from an entire academic unit and was library-centric, interoperable with a variety of systems, and extensible. This is not to say that TA was an intrinsically bad system; it was simply not right for Auraria Library.

Key Points

The selection of a streaming media system is not one to be taken lightly. As evidenced by this chapter's case study, myriad things can go wrong if not properly accounted for before investment. Even if a project team accounts for all envisioned eventualities, other things will arise that must be addressed. This is typical of an investment in any large-scale technology but is particularly true of streaming media systems, which are still in their adolescence. The key points of this chapter are as follows:

- It is very important to craft a list of desired qualities in a streaming system, but be sure to tailor these qualities to the institution in question, as some systems may seem ideal until stress-tested and applied locally.
- Popular streaming technologies are excellent ways to promote content not copyrighted by third parties and can be used to complement an authenticated streaming media system.
- Consideration of legal conditions of resources can make or break any effort to digitize and host audiovisual materials. It is important to understand the legalities of digitization before an investment in a technology is made.
- Trial and assess several systems, even if such a process takes several months, as a project team can typically make a better determination after having tested multiple technologies.

- Ask colleagues from other libraries and institutions what they use, and take into account the desires of constituents, as they may be able to point out things never imagined by a project team.
- Open the search for a streaming media system to other technologies that are capable of doing double duty with extensible features ready for future necessities.

Careful consideration of these points is crucial in selecting a streaming media solution. It is important to note that even if a solution is ideal, others may arise over the years that are even stronger and perhaps newly ideal. Anchoring to a system of any kind is unwise, as it limits possibilities for improvement and could ultimately damage the usability of a library's resources.

References

Internet Archive (IA). 2013. "Internet Archive Frequently Asked Questions." Archive.org. http://archive.org/about/faqs.php.

Vimeo. 2013. "Vimeo FAQ." https://vimeo.com/help/faq.

YouTube. 2013. "YouTube Privacy Settings." https://support.google.com/youtube/answer/157177?hl=en.

Enhancement and Promotion

MANY DECISIONS ARE MADE and resources expended in the process of simply digitizing an audiovisual collection, so it can be easy to become complacent when the core tasks of a project are completed. However, simply resting on these essential accomplishments will not behoove the overall usability and prominence of the final product. A collection, digitized or otherwise, must be promoted and enhanced in perpetuity, or at least a collection's promotion should be readdressed at regular intervals. Enhancement and promotion do not need to be extravagant or costly; the former can be as simple as adding robust metadata beyond what is normally required and the latter, a targeted "mini-campaign" aimed at a specific group of scholars. The intent is to maintain a collection's relevancy over time. So many digital projects are started, finished, and forgotten, often the victims of poor planning, insufficient funding, and slow lapses into irrelevance or obscurity.

Chapter 7 assembles the concepts of enhancement and promotion from examples of tools, programs, and methods for maintaining a collection's relevancy, first by exploring the overarching idea of relevancy, then by relating it through common tools. Enhancement and promotion are defined separately, but since they often complement each other or are achieved through the same processes, the tools discussed are holistic. These tools are easy to engage at any level and to wield at a minimum of expense. Much of the work of keeping up with changes in technology is done on the Internet, but there are many traditional methods for promotion that librarians can incorporate into their long-term project plans that are still effective, such as print advertising and meet-and-greets.

The idea of relevancy should never be confused with trendiness, which implies an eventual drop-off of recognition and importance. The core of relevancy is to be able to offer new perspectives on old (or older) data. These perspectives do not necessarily have to be novel or earth-shattering, but they should be appropriate to the material and enhance its usability and reach. By their nature, digital projects should be considered organic, which is to say they are never truly "completed." Static projects will certainly be useful to a segment of researchers for a period, but the way in which those projects are executed will eventually become stale. To be fair, there are many kinds of materials that will always maintain some level of relevancy by virtue of their natures, but their curation—the way that they are presented or related to other materials—is what draws new researchers and even the general public. Enhancing collections already established is an important step in achieving or maintaining relevancy.

Functional Enhancement

The enhancement of a digital audiovisual collection can take many forms, some inventive and unique, others common but tested. In either case, enhancements should never be purely topical or aesthetic and should always make the underlying mechanics of a project more effective and the top-level interactivity more useful. For the purposes of this book, an enhancement is an addition of dimension or mass, something added to a project that it did not previously have. Features—or dimensions—such as new metadata, closed captions, or subjectival geographic coordinates enhance the reach and usability of an object or collection by facilitating its interrelation with similar materials and projects. Even the simple addition of new materials—or mass—to a collection can be enough of a boost to maintain relevance by reaching critical mass, which is a way to establish a collection as authoritative and essential. The following value-added features are common assets of enhancement for many libraries, museums, and archives.

More and Better Metadata

Metadata are key to discovering learning resources and digital objects, whether through an online catalog or a search engine such as Google. Simply adding more metadata, though, is not always the best idea to increase something's findability. For example, a digitized VHS video about college student alcohol abuse would not benefit from the addition of dozens of simple terms, such as "drinking" or "alcohol," as such terms could easily relate to water, orange juice, or chemistry. Ambiguity is a problem in cataloging and can lead to poor search results or the accumulation of unrelated records. As Jeffrey Beall (2011) of the University of Colorado Denver puts it, "if you hear someone say, 'The shingles are in need of repair,' you innately know that shingles here refer to a roofing material and not an infectious disease." Humans are capable of making this distinction, but library catalogs and web search mechanisms are less capable; thus, it is up to the cataloger to be vigilant and attentive to the context of a resource.

However, extreme specificity can be just as damaging to an object. Overly specific metadata will exclude too much, disallowing serendipitous discovery of related materials. For example, when a person is browsing bookshelves for a certain item, he or she might stumble on better resources by virtue of accident, a phenomenon present only when subjects are literally close to one another. If each book were stored in its own library to maintain absolute specificity, the process of discovery would fail.

Ideally, metadata are both tailored and expansive. To achieve this target, librarians and archivists must work with catalogers to address individual items and sets of items intelligently with the end user in mind. In the previous example of a digitized VHS tape about college student alcohol abuse, the metadata creators would need to take into account the basic subjects, such as alcohol abuse, alcoholism, and college students, but they would also need to understand both the nature of the original medium and the persons interested in it. Such a video might be useful to a person interested in the construction and format of ephemeral films and instructional videos (see textbox 7.1); another might be interested in the dated perspectives of older videos on drug abuse; still others might simply be interested in archival educational films. To reach these kinds of individuals, simple subjective terms might not be sufficient.

TEXTBOX 7.1.

PROJECT STARTERS: MISCELLANEOUS UNIVERSITY FILMS AND VIDEOS

Description

A project centered on miscellaneous educational films may be one of the more exciting prospects that an archivist can pursue. So named, miscellaneous film and video collections contain smatterings of audiovisual material not easily categorized or not abundant enough in any one category to necessitate separation. Many university archives are replete with random VHS tapes, films, and audio materials whose provenance is not necessarily known. While they might be miscellaneous, there still ought to be a single thread connecting the items. One common thread, especially easy to find in a university archive, is educational media or instructional films. These materials could comprise videos by an academic department detailing the activities of a single course or even films of historical events produced by university personnel.

Common Sources

- University news and public affairs departments
- University audiovisual service units
- University journalism departments
- Nearly any university academic department
- University archives

Common Physical Formats

- VHS videocassettes
- U-Matic videocassettes
- Film (any gauge, most likely 16 mm)

(Continued)

Geography

It is easy to think of a digital object as a discrete unit of knowledge with no place other than within an intangible slice of a server. A silent film from the early twentieth century is both an object of entertainment and one of history. The 1916 film *Bouncing Baby* is a hidden gem of silent-era slapstick comedy and is recognized as such within the realms of filmic study. However, it can also be seen as a visual record of places and spaces. Shot entirely in Jacksonville, Florida, *Bouncing Baby* features views and scenery from downtown Jacksonville and nearby residential neighborhoods. As a visual artifact of the early twentieth century, *Bouncing Baby* (http://www.floridamemory.com/items/show/232392) is an excellent resource that could be useful to historical preservationists studying old buildings or local Florida historians interested in the way that Jacksonville has changed.

To make such a resource available to people researching the incidental contents of *Bouncing Baby* rather than its role as a comedy film, metadata creators would need to address the film from a spatial perspective rather than just a terminological one. It would be easy to just add such terms as "Jacksonville, Florida" or "historic downtowns" to the film's metadata, but while adding said metadata is important, also incorporating the object into a visual-spatial framework is ideal. For example, identifying points of interest in the film and assigning them standard geographic coordinates (e.g., latitude and longitude), a librarian can set the film and other related objects on a mapping product (e.g., Google Maps).

An excellent real-world example of a similar effort toward relating historical maps comes from the University of Florida, where antique and modern maps are coordinated

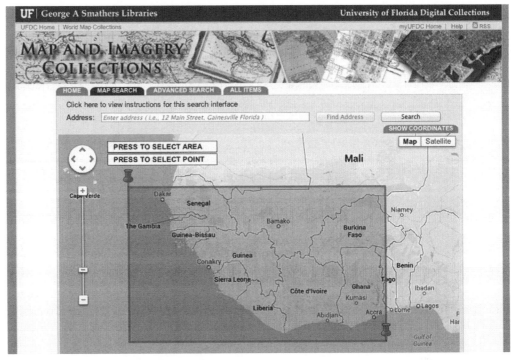

Figure 7.1. Map-Based Searching Enhancement.

to enhance collections. The Map and Imagery Digital Collections (http://ufdc.ufl.edu/maps/map) within the University of Florida Digital Collections (http://ufdc.ufl.edu) is enhanced with a map-based searching technology that allows users to drag squares around sections of a modern map (via Google Maps) to find all the maps within that area (see figure 7.1).

If a person drags a square around the lower third of the Caribbean basin, he or she will be presented with all the maps that fall within the chosen area. This technology could easily be wielded to showcase audiovisual materials that contain scenery of key locations, thus opening the study of those videos to a wider variety of researchers.

Closed Captioning and Transcription

Many audiovisual materials suffer from lack of accessibility features, such as closed captioning in videos or transcription of audio resources for the hearing impaired. Such features are important in creating inclusive collections that everyone can use, regardless of accessibility issues. Funding and labor can be roadblocks to transcribing audio or video objects, but all librarians involved in audiovisual digitization projects should do as much as they possibly can to overcome any hurdles to inclusiveness. In addition to making materials simply more accessible, transcripts and closed captions broaden the findability and research impact of videos and audios.

Transcripts are especially useful when trying to deepen the pool of terminology for creating metadata for a video. More is said or relayed through the audio stream of a video than what can always be ascertained by cursory viewings. Creating text-searchable transcripts of these audio streams, either through conversion of a subtitle file to plain text or by manual transcription, will allow researchers to search a video as they would a full-text PDF. Similarly, resources such as oral histories and audio interviews can be transcribed automatically or manually to produce searchable plain text that can be indexed and discovered through catalogs or search engines. Like optical character recognition software, which converts human-created text into machine-readable text, speech recognition software is not always precise. There are many costly software suites that a person can employ in automatically transcribing an audio file, but some open-source tools can be freely obtained, such as CMU Sphinx (http://cmusphinx.sourceforge.net) and Julius (http://julius.sourceforge.jp/en_index.php). However, though powerful and well regarded, such open-source solutions require programming support, and whatever is saved in money will be expended in staff time.

Better metadata, geographic context, and transcription are just a few possibilities that a librarian can explore when enhancing a digital collection. There are far too many options to explore in a single chapter; furthermore, not all value-adds will comply with every institution's standards and goals. Enhancing something does not simply mean adding features with abandon; it means calculating the correct features to add that complement the resources in question and do not require too much time, effort, and money to implement. Perhaps the most important thing to consider when making these kinds of judgments about collection enhancements is whether a value-add will do double duty as a functional feature and a promotional tool. This characteristic is preferable, especially concerning enhancements to digital collections that will do no good if not properly promoted and disseminated.

Promotion

Digital collections are services just like interlibrary loan programs, public catalogs, and journal subscriptions, but they do not always enjoy as much praise and use as the aforementioned. For a digital project to be successful, it must be promoted like any other product or service offered by a library, archive, or museum. Unlike many library services, digital collections tend to be created and launched with an unreasonable expectation that users will simply appear out of nowhere. This is rarely the case, though, perhaps because digital libraries are still somewhat novel and rely on constantly evolving standards and toolkits. In any case, advertising a collection's resources is advisable regardless of possible trends, as collections need attention to grow and promotion styles and methods can always be altered.

Naturally, like all other facets of a project, promotion will take a toll on a library's finances and/or its labor. It is wise to promote a collection to a specific group of potential users first, typically those with the most to gain from the collection's contents. If, for example, a group of archivists were to create a digital library from a digitized collection of agricultural educational films, it would certainly want to immediately inform any local agriculture, plant science, and animal science researchers of the collection's existence. When informed, these professors would be able to disseminate the collection to students and colleagues, thereby promoting it to a focused group. Ideally, local researchers (i.e., professors at an archivist's home institution) would be involved in the collection's creation from the beginning, but this is not always possible. As mentioned in chapter 4, collaboration with a professor or academic department can yield guaranteed usage of a new digital collection.

If a collection proves useful to a select group of interested persons, then it is safe to assume that wider promotion is a good idea. The following tools and methods can be employed to both promote digital audiovisual collections and enhance them. Special consideration is given to web-based products and services that offer social interaction and can be utilized by anyone, not just academics. Furthermore, consideration is offered to traditional marketing tools, such as print media and press releases, as they are still effective in bringing attention to collections and should not be dismissed as passé.

Basic Promotion

Digital collection managers should always consider wielding traditional marketing tactics and strategies to promote resources. Not every library or archive has an on-staff marketing professional, but there are many things that nonmarketers can do to help promote a digital collection. Before engaging in any kind of marketing, librarians and archivists in the position to make such decisions should first try to understand the environment in which they are operating. Tools such as SWOT (Strengths, Weaknesses, Opportunities, and Threats) can help project managers articulate and record the dimensions of this environment and how best to approach it. For example, if an audiovisual collection were digitized with the stipulation that its contents may be available to students only and not the general public, it would be a waste of effort to commit to a broad marketing campaign, which might confuse and disappoint peripheral library users.

If a digital collection is open to all potential users, print advertising (figure 7.2) in the form of pamphlets, postcards, or even full-sized posters is still an excellent way to market a resource. If key persons with vested interest in a collection were targeted with e-mail and face-to-face meetings, print materials are a good way to begin reaching out to

Figure 7.2. Postcard Advertisement for Digital Collection.

students and the general public. Print materials can be carried away and can act as tangible reminders that a resource is available electronically or at a physical location. Even though people are constantly connected to the Internet, there are few things as immediate as walking by a large, full-color poster of a possibly invaluable and interesting event or resource.

If wider attention is required, press releases are a good way to insert the story of a collection into local print media, such as newspapers or, on a smaller but perhaps more effective scale, university-wide newsletters. Library professionals at Old Dominion University in Norfolk, Virginia, had relative success promoting their collections through both print materials and an e-mail-based newsletter with more than three hundred subscribers, mostly faculty, staff, and students (Cole, Graves, and Cipkowski 2010). While three hundred subscribers to a newsletter may seem paltry, it is unwise to misunderstand the place of a library or digital collection. Either will likely never see the same level of attention as a service such as YouTube, but it is unreasonable to expect such results in the first place. Libraries should strive toward critical use of collections, not just quantity.

Finally, even something as simple as a link on a commonly visited website, such as a library's homepage or research portal, will likely reach an even greater number of potential users, especially if that link is placed near other links with high click rates. While quantity should never be the sole metric by which a collection is assessed, the more users that a resource attracts, the more chances (i.e., serendipitous discovery) that arise for the right individual to see a resource and benefit from it wholly. This approach can either complement or be complemented by what are commonly referred to as Web 2.0 tools, services such as Twitter, Facebook, and YouTube. While not all of these tools are totally effective, the right combination of them specific to whatever project is being promoted can help broaden user bases and serve as promotional tools.

YouTube

YouTube (http://www.youtube.com) is a powerful tool for promotion and dissemination of audiovisual materials but has some drawbacks that may not be suitable for some collections. YouTube is ideal for complementing a streaming video system (as discussed in chapter 6) because it is unmatched in terms of number of users and cultural proliferation. According to YouTube, more than one billion unique users visit its site each month and watch more than six billion hours of video in that time (YouTube 2013). If the main concern of a project team is access to viewers, YouTube is the best place to host content. However, just because a video is on the world's most popular video-hosting service does not mean that it will be viewed by thousands of people. Successful promotion of videos through YouTube includes focused metadata and tagging paired with traditional marketing methods such as print advertising.

Where YouTube is less desirable is in the promotion and dissemination of culturally sensitive materials. While audience pool is effectively unlimited, materials that could be easily misinterpreted due to a cultural misunderstanding will be open to a greater array of negativity. Even though comments made on a video can be prohibited or moderated, YouTube's commercial and highly popularized leaning may not be the best place to host videos that can be easily misunderstood. For example, the University of Florida Digital Library Center was involved in a project to collect and preserve videos showing rarely seen ceremonies performed by practitioners of Haitian Vodou, sometimes referred to as "Voodoo." Vodou is a widely misunderstood and maligned religion, and upon embarking on the archiving and hosting of videos of sacred Vodou practice, the project team was highly concerned with the proper platform. YouTube, because of its reach and ease of use, was initially used, and the videos received much attention. However, after a stream of negative and disparaging comments, as well as the inherent difficulties in separating academic videos in YouTube from parodies and entertainment, it was decided that You-Tube was not appropriate. In lieu of a retail or in-house streaming system, the Digital Learning Center opted for using a YouTube-similar but education-centered service called Vimeo.

YouTube is best at hosting archival audiovisual resources that do not require authentication (as discussed in chapter 6) or are absent culturally sensitive or potentially offensive content. Among such acceptable resources are

- University news and public affairs videos
- Library training videos
- Archived course lectures
- Speeches and lectures

Each library will have its own requirements and may interpret the concept of cultural sensitivity differently, but project managers should strive to be aware of any and all potential hurdles to a collection's proper and responsible handling. There are many freely available web-based tools that are designed around restrained—or specialized—curation, a practice that helps to mitigate concerns of sensitivity and appropriateness.

Internet Archive

Founded in 1996 by archivist and entrepreneur Brewster Kahle, Internet Archive (IA; http://www.archive.org) is one of the world's leading free and open resources for digitized human knowledge. IA's mission is to be a repository for all manner of human creativity, data, and information that is freely accessible to anyone (IA 2013). In 2012, IA celebrated the accumulation of 10 petabytes (a petabyte equals 1,000 terabytes) of data, including texts, rare books, magazines, and audiovisual files (Drinehart 2012). While IA can be used to freely and simply host most any kind of data, it is particularly good at storing audiovisual material and allowing for its effective curation.

For most users, the 10-gigabyte page size limit is not a concern. For clarification purposes, IA considers one page (see figure 7.3) as a single item, whether it incorporates a single file or two dozen.

For all video objects, IA creates a series of derivatives, or versions, each with a specific set of users in mind. For example, a high-resolution MPEG4 is suitable for download and presentation on large screens; a 512-kb MPEG4 is best for viewing on slower connections or mobile devices; and an MPEG2 is best for storing and distributing on a DVD or similar medium. Part of promoting and enhancing an audiovisual collection is making it as easily and widely usable as possible, and this usually means creating enough derivative files to satisfy a variety of users. IA's system automatically produces these derivatives, which, for the most part, should be usable by the largest cross section of individuals.

Once a content contributor has uploaded fifty pages (fifty individual items with distinct titles), he or she is allowed to create a unique collection that will exist alongside the hundreds of curated collections already in IA. A unique collection allows administrators to

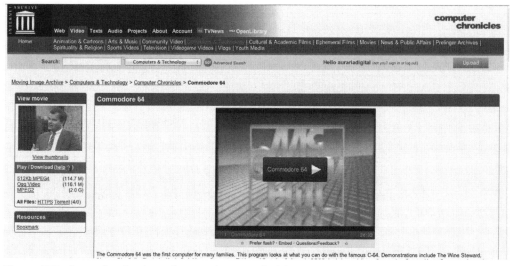

Figure 7.3. Example of an Item Page on Internet Archive.

curate large amounts of data based on subject, content, or any other characteristic. Furthermore, unlike YouTube, IA has a predominantly academic or, rather, non-entertainment-focused audience. Many institutions use IA to complement their digital repositories, while some, because of IA's large storage capacity and freeness, use IA to store the entirety of their collections. The reputation and historical usage of IA ensures that a variety of serious users will go to IA seeking curated content, such as episodes of an early 1990s television show about the Internet, the historical archives of ARPANET, or collections of ephemeral films from the 1940s.

For all its richness in variety and accommodation of curation, IA lacks the visual appeal and much-sought Web 2.0 features of other tools. Whether a philosophical choice or technological limitation imposed by some other factor, IA has focused more on accumulation and inclusion than on creative presentation. Luckily, there are other tools that can complement the very same resources that are stored in IA or other repositories that have the same commitment to accessibility.

Historypin

Created by a United Kingdom–based nonprofit called We Are What We Do, Historypin (http://www.historypin.com) is a web-based sharing tool allowing anyone to upload and "pin" photographs and videos to a certain place and time (Historypin 2013). Users of this tool are encouraged to upload old family photographs and films, placing them on a specific point on a Google-powered map that can be searched by term, location, and year. Among Historypin's many features is a rephotography option that allows users to align old photographs of buildings or streets with new imagery captured through Google's Streetview system. Many academic institutions use Historypin to augment their photography collections or create rich audiovisual tours of a historical location. For example, were an archivist to upload to Historypin a few dozen images of random persons and sites from Denver, Colorado, he or she could use it as a way to encourage the general public to contribute its own relevant images and videos. The term *crowdsourcing* is a bit overused, but in such a case where the public is engaged in a location-driven exploration of history, it is an appropriate concept.

Whether simply a value-add or an excellent tool for encouraging collaboration and contribution to a collection, Historypin should not serve as a simple repository. Historypin, like many other augmentative tools, is best when wielded as a lure to bring persons to a larger, more complex repository or even to the physical archive itself. Historypin enforces a 5-megabyte size limit on photographs, which does not allow for high-resolution images, and both audio and video items must be in YouTube before they can be pinned (Historypin 2013). These restraints are reasonable given the site's partnership with Google (which owns YouTube) but may be discouraging for persons that do not use YouTube or wish to present only the highest-resolution images possible.

Historypin's usefulness as a promotional tool, though, despite its technological limitations regarding image size and video hosting, cannot be overstated. Like most of the promotional tools discussed in this chapter, Historypin can also be seen as an enhancer, or feature addition. It is not promoted by its creators as a one-stop digital repository solution, and it should not be mistaken for such. Historypin, YouTube, and IA cannot do everything for everyone, but they work well as components to a larger, more complex toolbox. The fact that these services are free is perhaps the most compelling reason for a librarian or archivist to at least attempt to use them, but they are widely used and explored by millions of persons.

Ⓖ Key Points

Enhancing and promoting digital audiovisual collections need not be an arduous process, nor should it be one in which thousands of hours are invested. Some promotional tactics and strategies simply do not work, and the reasons for failure are not necessarily obvious. It is important to be flexible, understand key audiences, and consider the limitations of digitized content. With the exception of printed marketing materials such as posters and handouts, the tools discussed in this chapter are all free, and should they prove inappropriate for a collection, disengagement is simple and costless. However, if these tools prove useful and yield measurable results in the use of a digital collection, they can be wielded in perpetuity and, in many cases, integrated with other tools, such as Drupal, WordPress, or proprietary repository software. Planning for the promotion and enhancement of digital collection can be approached as an individual effort or incorporated into a larger, institution-wide marketing plan. In either case, the most important thing to remember is that users need to be able to get the most out of a resource, whether it is visited by ten thousand persons or just fifty.

The key points in enhancement promotion of digital audiovisual collections are as follows:

- Account for promotion during the initial stages of project planning. Doing so will lessen the possibility of a collection becoming stale.
- Assess each project's needs individually—what works for one collection will not always work for another, and assuming the opposite can result in wasted effort.
- Do not be afraid to change gears during a promotional campaign—there are too many constantly changing factors to consider that being married to concept can be a setup for failure.
- Avoid tools that are exclusionary to persons with disabilities or do not permit viewing to certain segments of society.

- Make use of free tools and services, as their engagement will require only labor and not money, which is not always readily available.
- Consider users in succession from most specific to most general. If a collection is deemed highly useful to a certain group of researchers, students, or academic units, it is safe to assume that it will be for similar sectors external to the institution—or even the general public.
- Do not underestimate the effectiveness of print media—it is still a part of human life and can reach a wider variety of potential users.
- Avoid rigidity in a marketing plan, and favor a marketing concept that can be altered with minimal effort.
- Keep abreast of changes in technology, metadata, marketing, and web tools and incorporate new ideas when necessary, but do not shift course solely based on newness of a trend.

Careful consideration of these points is essential in crafting a successful approach to marketing and enhancing digital audiovisual collections, broadening user bases, and ensuring relevancy.

References

Beall, J. 2011. "Academic Library Databases and the Problem of Word-Sense Ambiguity." *Journal of Academic Librarianship* 37, no. 1: 64–69.

Cole, K., T. Graves, and P. Cipkowski. 2010. "Marketing the Library in a Digital World." *Serials Librarian* 58, nos. 1–4: 182–87.

Drinehart. 2012. "10,000,000,000,000,000 bytes archived!" *Internet Archive Blogs* (blog). October 26. http://blog.archive.org/2012/10/26/10000000000000000-bytes-archived/.

Historypin. 2013. "Frequently Asked Questions. 'We Are What We Do.'" Historypin.com. http://www.historypin.com/faq/.

Internet Archive (IA). 2013. "About the Internet Archive." http://archive.org/about/.

YouTube. 2013. "Statistics." http://www.youtube.com/yt/press/statistics.html.

Essential Takeaways

AS THE PRECEDING CHAPTERS SHOW, the challenges of starting an audiovisual digitization program from the ground up are myriad but soluble. As is the case with many new ventures for librarians and information professionals, audiovisual digitization is perhaps intimidating because it is simply unfamiliar. It is hoped that after reading *Managing Digital Audiovisual Resources*, librarians and allied professionals will be able to comfortably and confidently embark on an audiovisual digitization venture or perhaps just buttress their developing program with fresh information and perspectives.

Successive readings of this book will prove useful, but there are some essential takeaways that readers should absorb as they reflect on the material in preparation for further readings. The takeaways refer to specific topics covered in previous chapters and serve as digestible overviews of the most important facets of audiovisual digitization and resource management.

⊚ Essential Takeaways

Managing Digital Audiovisual Resources begs five essential takeaways. With these concepts in mind, readers will be able to consider their comprehension of this book and the object of its intent a success.

Reliance on the Experiences of Others

The first takeaway—and perhaps the most important thing to remember about audiovisual resources and their digitization—is that no person is ever alone in his or her frustrations or victories. Dozens of archivists and librarians are likely engaged in projects similar to your own and are experiencing the same issues or have already solved them. It is important to seek out other professionals and consult them. While audiovisual digitization may not be as well recorded as other aspects of the library world, there are many examples or workflows, processes, and tactics that a person will discover if he or she seeks them out. Qualitative research and anecdotal evidence abounds in this field, so it is equally important that while you solicit help for an issue, you ought to record your own experiences.

Knowledge of Collections

Much of this book is concerned with the identification of material types and the effective differences among types of collections. The second takeaway—knowledge of collections and how to interact with different materials—is important on a technical level, but more crucial than understanding what makes a U-Matic tape different from a VHS cassette is the wherewithal to see importance where it may not be obvious. This level of understanding is essential in delivering a quality product to your constituents—students, professors, and laypersons alike. Fascinating and useful materials can languish in obscurity because of disuse, but in most cases, it is simply that such objects have never been given due consideration or were advertised relative to their importance. The job of the audiovisual curator is equal parts understanding materials and understanding the significance of their holdings—and getting others to understand the same.

Importance of Planning

Chapters 2 and 3 delve into the physicality of materials as well as the necessity for planning, which is the third takeaway. If there is a single thing that a librarian can do to ensure the solidity of a project, it is to thoroughly plan a project and document that plan. As noted several times in this book, planning does not ensure success, but it certainly eliminates questions of sincerity and readiness, should a project falter. To be sure, though, success should be assumed at the outset; confidence goes a long way in delivering satisfying results.

Comprehending Materials

The fourth takeaway is a greater understanding of the inner workings of materials. This book delves deep enough into the technical aspects of audiovisual formats and equipment to help professionals think seriously about the logistics of such a venture. Much of the necessary equipment is difficult to obtain and maintain, but the value of controlling your own processes from tape to digital file is so high that it makes any hurdles worth overcoming. That said, some individuals may have no desire to field equipment of that ilk and are more interested in the content of the tapes than control over digitization. Even in cases where librarians need only to send material to a vendor, they must still have a basic understanding of what it is they are requesting. Sincere attempts at understanding concepts out of your realm go a long way in proving commitment to a project.

Manage the Product

The fifth takeaway demands remembering that a project does not end when materials have been digitized. It does not end when digital files are put online and access is technically provided. It does not even end when there are simply no more tapes to capture and present. A digital project might be bounded at first but can always be expanded. Expansion and development are what separates relevant digital libraries and projects from irrelevant ones. It is easy to become excited about completing a project, especially one rife with trouble, but doing so puts the entire venture at risk of becoming just another silo of data with no life. There are many ways to enliven stale projects, but the expansion and development of an audiovisual digitization effort should be built into the core plan. With development in mind from the beginning of a project, it will be much easier to carry on with improvements and enhancements as time progresses. Enhancements do not necessarily have to be technological, either, and can come in the form of collaborations with local teaching faculty and even other libraries. Taking old information and interpreting it in new ways lies at the very heart of digital humanities, and audiovisual resources lend themselves well to display, enhancement, and reinterpretation.

Final Takeaway

The practice of effective management of digital audiovisual resources comes more from experience than anything else. The simple act of declaring that, for example, a collection of VHS tapes shall be digitized and made available to an interested audience is nearly all that is required to start a project. Documentation, equipment acquisition, and other logistical and administrative tasks will fall in line with the application of effort at the correct stages of a project. A person should never be fearful of failure at a project's outset, but one should be aware that if attention is not given to the essential concepts of digitization management, the difficulty of attaining success increases. The best mind-set that a librarian can have is positivity, as confidence in a project's intent and its constituent parts will become apparent in the final product and lead to success.

Index

migration, 4, 8, 61, 108. *See also* preservation
motion JPEG 2000, 87
motion picture film, 21–22
MOV, 28, 30, 90
MP3, 31
MP4. *See* MPEG-4
MPEG-2, 29
MPEG-4, 28–29

National Digital Information Infrastructure and
    Preservation Program (NDIIP), 87

Old Dominion University, 118

PCM (pulse code modulation), 84, 85
permission letters, 62–63
phonograph records, 18–19
platform agnosticism, 87, 95
playback devices, 71–78; marketplaces for, 78–79
preservation: digital, 28, 33–34, 41; physical, 11, 40–41.
    See also Library of Congress
print advertising, 117–18
public domain, 60

quarter-inch tape. *See* reel-to-reel
QuickTime, 28, 30

RCA cable, 79
RealAudio, 33
records. *See* phonograph records
reel-to-reel tape, 17–18; players, 75–77

S-Video cable, 80
Society of Motion Picture and Television Engineers
    (SMPTE), 87
software: basics of, 83; capture, 84; transcoders, 83–84

special collections, 6–7
standards for digitization, 85–88
Stanford University Media Preservation Lab, 7, 86
storage: of digital materials, 52, 70, 87, 95; of physical
    materials, 41
streaming media systems: case study on, 106–9;
    platforms, 98–106; qualities of, 94–95
surveying collections, 38–41

technological support, 45, 53
transcription, 115–16
TRS cable, 79

U-Matic, 15–16; VCR, 74
University of Florida: and course integration, 57–58; and
    cross-institutional collaboration, 58; and culturally
    sensitive materials, 118–19; historical mapping, 114–15
University of Michigan Library Digital Conversion Unit,
    69

vendors, 67–68; communicating with, 69–70; selection
    of, 69
VHS, 12–13; in circulating collections, 7–8; players,
    72–73
Vimeo, 100–101

Waveform Audio File Format (WAV), 31–32
Windows Media Audio (WMA), 32
Windows Media Video (WMV), 31
workflows, digitization: audio only, 88–89; audiovisual,
    89–90

XLR cable, 80

YouTube: as promotional tool, 118–19; as streaming
    platform, 99–100

About the Author

Matthew C. Mariner was born and raised in St. Petersburg, Florida. After junior college, he moved to Gainesville to attend the University of Florida, where he received a bachelor of arts in English. Shortly after receiving his undergraduate degree, Matthew worked for the University of Florida Digital Library Center, managing the institutional repository and overseeing the center's preservation, archiving, and optical character recognition programs. While employed at the university, Matthew earned his master of historic preservation degree. Currently, he resides in Denver, Colorado, with his wife and two cats and serves as the head of Special Collections and Digital Initiatives at Auraria Library, a tri-institutional academic library in downtown Denver.